A YEAR OBSERVED

A YEAR OBSERVED

WILSON STEPHENS

Sketches by Mary Beattie Scott

PELHAM BOOKS

First published in Great Britain by
Pelham Books Ltd
44 Bedford Square
London WC1B 3DU
1984

British Library Cataloguing in Publication Data

Stephens, Wilson
    A year observed.
    1. Great Britain——Social life and customs
    ——1945- 2. Great Britain——Rural
    conditions
    I. Title
    941'.009'734 DA588

ISBN 0 7207 1541 5

Typeset, printed and bound in Great Britain
by Butler and Tanner Ltd, Frome, Somerset and London

'Yet between life and death are hours
To flush with love and hide in flowers;
What profit save in these?' men cry:

'Ah, see, between soft earth and sky,
What only good things here are ours!''

For Marygold

FINALE IN PLACE
OF A PRELUDE

NOW that I have told the story of a year in the country, I can remember how simple the enterprise appeared when first attempted. The months and the seasons, the rhythms of life renewing and life receding, the ebb and flow of human activity, would impose their own pattern of its unfolding. In practice, it was otherwise.

A thousand ages in Thy sight is but an evening gone. So we sing in a hymn. A year looked back upon proves to be a very minor fraction of time, so small as to be all one piece, and indivisible.

So the story is told accordingly, as it happened to me in its trivia and truths. In the end there is no such thing as time, only experience.

LIFE has made me a Winter man. Summer's pleasures are mainly idle times, so of diminished interest, and much dependent on solar radiation. For years the sun did its best to incinerate me in climates where it is more foe than friend. Now I prefer the touch of the wind, blowing over my home country, bringing to me the living message of wild exhalations – flowers and tree sap, breath of new-turned furrows, fume of heather blooming, reek of slurry reinforcing fertility, new hay, antiseptic crispness of frost. Wind, not sunshine, governs weather. The good English wind is at its best in Winter.

Livelier air summons up the blood, quickens the pace, sharpens perceptions, widens the view. I can see where I am going. Landscapes laid bare among leafless trees, their life retracted to minimum, can hide little of themselves. Home truths stand out clearly. One of them is that Winter, as many of us think of it, nihilistic in its suspension of vitality, is a very short interlude. Most of Winter is a time of resurgence. The Winter of Christmas cards and tradition – white, virginal, barren – is not Winter as we know it. When Winter is most reviled, and its denominator is not snow but mud, life is in the ascendant again. Winter is more alpha than omega.

From the nothingness of the dead of the year, the resurrection is wonderfully swift. Only a few days separate the end of all things from a fresh start. The infallible punctuality of Nature is so easily overlooked that most people see Spring, not Winter, as the time of upsurge; Spring when lambs play in the fields at

Easter, with primroses and daffodils blooming. This pleasant illusion contains both truth and falsehood. The synchronised arrivals of lambs, feats of obstetrics organised on a multiple scale, are the countryside's greatest visible re-population explosions. But these actual happenings are seldom truly part of Spring. The reality could scarcely be less vernal, there being no place where the facts of life are more stark than in a lambing pen, in full production, in February.

The wind is not always welcome, of course. Sometimes it is an ordeal for man and beast as when, on this harsh day of a freezing northerly, the face of Winter steel-grim across earth and sky, four of us are in action there. Three hundred and fifty ewes are delivering, just one batch on a big farm high on the Wessex uplands. Here, where the wool clip made the wealth of medieval England, the bare and rolling hills are still the setting where shepherds watch their flocks by night. Today we do more than merely watch.

"We're knee deep in lambs already," the farmer said this morning, "and more coming thick and fast." He could do with more hands. I have two, unskilled but available and, Winter being when the action is, I lend them. He himself has greater matters to attend to. He says he is proud of us, and leaves us to it.

Together we express the changed face of rural England. Malcolm, the shepherd, aged twenty-two, stocky and bearded, with the improbable accents of London's West End; Tracey, the same age, strapping and dark haired, has a Gloucestershire burr; Ron, whose oaken country face splits easily into mirth, is sixteen. So they, the three technicians, have a combined age of sixty – that at which a single traditional "shep" of the old school would have been regarded a generation ago as having just about got the hang of the job. I can give them a few years, but I am not skilled. I can grease an arm for somebody else when quick action is needed, kick the generator into life when light fades, hay up the creeps, bring in the first-borne with their dams, keep them watered and (in due priority) make the tea. But these are mere chores, significant only because if I did not do them the others

would have to. By being here, I free them for real work.

This farm sets its sights high. The expectation is that, on average, every ewe shall go out to pasture the mother of twins, which means seven hundred healthy lambs, most of them within three days and nights. But the hope and aim are for something better – not just that no ewe goes out except with twins, but as many as possible with triplets, pushing the total as near as we can get it to a thousand. This involves past, present and future. It depends on the fertility bred into the sheep by ancestry, a minimum failure rate at lambing, and no losses in rearing. So far we have had few failures, but are less than half-way through.

The northerly has a knife-edge to it. It wails over the rear of the double-span barn across which a wall of straw bales has been built. In the lee of this the air is still but not cosy. Sheep are the best clad of all creatures, and new-born lambs must not go soft through luxury. Their destiny, within a few days, is out of doors in winds as cruel as that now blowing. In this Spartan place those already born are now as snug with their mothers as they will ever be, each in her individual pen.

The ewes which have not yet lambed, more than two hundred of them, wait in a hurdled space beyond the barn's open front, out of the wind but under no cover except the hard grey sky. The ground is thickly strawed. They are calm, unworried, but pack close together, united by the universal tie of maternity. In the presence of this all-pervading force, some accepted fallacies correct themselves.

Most of us think that life begins with birth. The truth is that life itself never ends, though the vehicles in which it is carried wear out; ourselves, for instance. Individual beings take distinct form when their parents copulate, their potentialities thereafter alterable only for the worse. Parturition is the first hurdle in a life already in progress for months. We inherit our characters, but not our destinies, as sheep inherit theirs. Sheep, as expressions of the human condition, familiar in religion and made more valid where socialism spreads, loom larger here as examples of what cloning could do.

This flock are Scotch half-breds, sired by Border Leicester

rams on Cheviot dams. Compared with other sheep, their hybrid vigour gives them the look of thoroughbreds – big, with a proud upstanding bearing, their great Roman noses implying aloofness from lesser examples of their kind. Hybrid vigour also gives them fertility in procreation, especially when tupped by pure-bred Suffolk rams, as these have been. On such fusions of ovine blood rest the hopes of a lamb crop exceeding two hundred per cent.

The policy is laid down by the farmer, a traditional flockmaster for whom sheep are as faith to a priest. Malcolm carries it out. Things go quiet, as they often do when the sun is in the descendant and the whole tempo of life takes its time accordingly, and he finds time to talk. He had a weekend's leave before lambing began, and chats of London to Tracey who has been there once, and to Ron who never has. Malcolm comes of a musical family. His parents (with singular lack of influence on his future) both play classical music in top orchestras. His breeding is by a cellist out of a flautist. Tracey says "Fancy that!" Ron wanders off. We hear him reversing a tractor, going to pick up hay.

Malcolm enjoys music, but his bond with sheep is deeper. The greatest artistic pleasure palls when you live with it on all sides, day-in day-out. So he wanted to be on the land, and went through agricultural college after a year and a half "practical". He came to sheep by a process of elimination. Dairying, like music, is another day-in day-out life, never much change from season to season. He dislikes pigs. And he had little taste for tractors, and the other more complex implements which now do cultivation. That left only sheep. He found them good company, not such fools as people think them. You had to be in love with sheep if you were to make a go of them.

At peak period, before the drafts begin going to market, he has about two and a half thousand to look after. He does it single-handed, except at lambing time, and with occasional part-time help. Yes, some of the shepherds on other farms round about do think him a bit odd. They think the governor is even more odd for giving him the job. He thinks it a good life. Every now and then he has a few days off. Then he puts on his London clothes, and drives his sports car up to the smoke. That keeps his hand in for the other kind of life. He does not know if he will ever go back to it. He is happy. Now is now. Why look ahead?

He and I check on the artificial twinning, which is not an instant process. Some strong ewes produce only one live lamb, yet have plenty of milk. So weak lambs from triple births are fostered on to them. The problem is in persuading the ewe to take over a lamb which is not her own. It needs quick decision. While her own lamb is still wet from afterbirth, with all the attendant odours on it, a dry lamb from an earlier birth is often accepted. By contact with each other, the two soon carry the same scent, and she cannot tell them apart. Ewes differ in their maternal instinct. One reason for single penning is that some will steal the lambs of other ewes. Others accept, then change their minds. Malcolm's quick eye and methodical mind achieves the share-out little by little. The price of the twinning average is eternal vigilance.

Light fades. Ron returns, hay-up completed. He and Malcolm zip their anoraks, mount the tractor and roar away to the village. They will sleep six hours before returning and taking over for the second half of the night. I brew up. Tracey has a nice line in chocolate bars, and there is a large communal tin of sandwiches. We feel well provisioned for our time on watch.

We watch, literally, from a vantage point. More straw bales are stacked against the back wall to form a miniature grandstand. From it we can see across the rows of individual pens to the flock of waiting ewes beyond. The generator-powered roof lights are not of operating-theatre intensity, but we know what

13

we are looking for against the background of darkness thickening outside.

Tracey is a disciplined chain-smoker. Through the afternoon she lit a cigarette after every lamb. Now she has a small tin beside her in which she dutifully stubs each glowing butt. I presume this to be within the rules, say nothing, and listen to the story of her life – agricultural college, her boyfriend on an oil rig, the new job she is to start when this has finished, her special role here in charge of intensive care. There are times, as in all births, when lambs hang between death and life. These borderline cases are her concern. She can do what a ewe cannot, exercise a bit of intelligence. If she gets a still breathing "marginal" into her hospital down at the farm, its survival prospects change from odds against to near certainty.

The change from day to night is now total, and things liven up again. Ewe after ewe quits the huddled mass outside, walks uneasily round for a minute or so, then lies down with head held high – alert, disturbed, anticipatory. Then labour begins, and our twinning rate and triplet hopes are at stake.

Sometimes it is difficult to tell, from the movements of the body under the wool, the precise moment when a lamb is born. The angle of the ewe's head, the curve and flexing of the neck as maternal licking starts, are the give-away. Then the mother is eased up on to her feet and follows her infant, carried ahead, into a pen of their own. By the time she arrives there Tracey knows the form. "Another one to come, maybe two," she says. Priorities now need arranging.

If the ewe can deliver the remaining lambs unaided, so much the better. But multiple lambings must not take too long. If they do, the later lambs risk death from drowning in a womb flooded with placenta liquid already released by the internal bursting of the embryonic sac. Dead lambs are commonplace in hill flocks, where there is no human aid. Our task is to see that there are no dead lambs here. Tracey – "by skill and sense and strength of arm" – gets the timing right for a dozen lambs in a row. Sandwiches seem a long way off. We deal with raw life and its accompaniments, the fight for breath, the reek of disinfectant and of blood. Eventually the synchronisation slips. I, too, must link my fingers round forelegs, match the heavings, elbow in flank, give the decisive extra force and earn the triumph of seeing the lamb lie wet and slippery, steaming in the bitter air.

Just a ray of life, elongated like a fish, sodden, blood-smeared, collapsed. It is a moment we have all survived. I rub my hand up its length a time or two, jerking it towards existence. It is warm – but then it would be, wouldn't it? Hope, banal as it was, forthwith dies. More rubs, a snuffled sneeze, and it breathes. The breath of life makes the rib cage swell and cave in unevenly until, after gasps and stutters, it holds a steady rhythm. Up comes the narrow, snake-like head, turning inquiringly this way and that as if the lamb, only two minutes "old", had already mislaid something. The search is quickly over. It has found its mother's udder, and sucks. Milk begins to fill the tissues that were dehydrated for the journey into light and air.

"Singleton?" asks Tracey, a dry lamb over her arm. "Twin," I answer. "Sod it," she says, "I want a wet singleton for this little beggar, and soon."

Just another lamb; no great event for the professionals, but quite a moment for me. I move on. There will be more, and more and more. I see the worth of Tracey, her off-hand determination, hard-boiled expertise, and a touch too sure to come from anything but caring.

The tempo slackens. "No panic for a bit," she says, drawing and puffing cigarette smoke as if it were life-support oxygen. "They always come in bursts; now we'll have half an hour easy." We dip our arms biceps-deep into a water trough which, surprisingly, has not frozen. Dried-off, we get busy with kettle, sandwich-tin, and chocolate bars. I have some sloe gin, which does not last long. We sit on the straw-bale grandstand for ten minutes. Then Tracey goes to check on the fosterings, including her latest problem case for which a wet singleton has turned up just in time. I walk slowly and watchfully

15

among the waiting ewes, in case lambs have been born that we know nothing about.

Out here, under the sky, the whiplash wind is as merciless as ever. But it has cleared the clouds. Overhead is a dome of stars, diamond-bright in the purity of empty night. Below them, and all around are clusters of light, earth's own constellations. They are the camps and villages spread across the plain below where men are drinking or playing snooker, and well-warmed families sit tight around television sets. To the South a red dot hangs low in the sky. It is the aircraft warning light on Salisbury Cathedral spire. The human race goes about its twentieth century affairs. We have been back to the dawn of time.

Three days later the lambs born that bitter night are out on the open down. The same wind blows, emptying the scene of other life. No larks sing, no pipits fly, nor finches forage for last autumn's spilled seed. The tumbling peewits are down in the vale, where moist ground near the river still takes a probing bill. The jack hares that court their fancies and box off rivals when Spring is in their blood have no such thoughts yet, and stay snug in woodland. Only the sheep behave as if that wind did not blow, somebody having rightly said that there is no substitute for wool.

Already the lamb families are joining up in groups of eight or ten to skip and run races, and practise cornering at speed, as do the young of many species, including ours. The ewes lie peacefully, backs windward, forming small enclaves of shelter to which the lambs return to suck and rest. This rugged introduction is probably the last hard weather they will see. By August all of them will have fulfilled their destiny via the dinner plates of the nation, including many of those who rhapsodised over watching their brief joy in life. Among them may also be some who, having enjoyed their mutton, deplore that pheasants are reared "only to be slaughtered" as human food, and become holier-than-thou at the contemplation of the likes of me.

But such is Fate, even for those creatures of which we take the greatest care. Second generation cross-bred sheep are no use for breeding. Each of their generations must be created separately by a new union of Leicester rams on Cheviot ewes, and a fresh intervention of Suffolks. Sheep can be bred in many different ways, but the marketable version are seldom long in this world. Even parent stock last only as long as their commercial attributes – ewes while their teeth, udders and feet are serviceable, rams until virility fades.

A ewe could hope for six or seven years of life, a ram for four or five, if they were capable of hoping, which they are not – nor of mourning their foreshortened existence. Old age is unknown in farm stock. How long ewes and rams (or cows and bulls, sows and boars) might live if they were pensioned off is hence unknown. Long ago I saw a bunch of venerable Romney Marsh ewes keeping tidy a Kentish orchard which, the owner said, they had been doing since the time of his father then twenty years dead. They were the oldest sheep I ever saw, or am likely to see.

A far cry, of course, from relative cosiness under the apple trees to the exposure of these lean heights. We are on the 600-foot contour here, where the land has never been fenced, and only recently ploughed. It has its own wild freedom, its own ancient history. Here, when darkness falls and men go home to cottages on the valley floor, its sparse populations re-assemble much as they did before the Druids came. Foxes can run straight-necked for miles with no need to make detours round villages. With the dusk, roe-deer move uphill from blackthorn hangers on the lower slopes. Partridges jug in sheltered hollows. They are in pairs at this time of year, and each cock calls a last "tizzick" to his neighbour at last light. Owl voices come up from the lusher levels. There is little up here to keep mice alive or, by association, owls alive either.

FINE days give a far view to gentler regions. Beyond the high-lying plain, its lines still broken by the collapsed tombs and temples of ancient peoples, still scarred by their trackways, wooded lowlands are in sight. The dead grey primary hue of winter landscape changes to the umber of fertility where the plough has been, the fields divided by those familiar barriers, hedges. But for how much longer?

In East Anglia the immemorial elm trees and hedges alike have already disappeared over miles-long tracts of land. The elms were killed by beetles from Holland. The hedges have been torn up to enable the juggernaut power of modern farming to be worked with less interruption, hence more economically. The effect is land without wind-breaks, which means land with less fertility, land lacking shelter, land without warmth.

Here in Wessex, where the rolling hills and steep vales preclude prairie-type high-speed and high-powered farming, most hedges remain. This was never specifically elm tree country, so hedgerow trees of other species still stand. But the prospect twenty years hence is another matter. I fear the change to a more naked countryside is coming; indeed, coming to all Britain south and east of the stone-wall districts. Where large-scale mechanisation does not dictate this, small-scale mechanisation will make it inevitable. The change, now proceeding inexorably at Nature's own pace, is both cause and effect of the different way of life on the land. We four in the lambing pen expressed it.

Land people are as distinctive a community as seafarers. Both are changing in the same way. Hands, with their varied skills, are being replaced by apparatus. The degree to which the land can be served is limited to what machines can do. Machines are non-adaptable, crude by comparison with craftsmanship. The last generation of skilled farm hands are now seeing their role passing to similarly skilled mechanics and, by neither's fault, the land they served in danger.

Ron, the all-round lad who knows the needs of the moment and turns his hand accordingly without waiting to be told, would have become one of the old school when the experience of years had ripened all his talents. Malcolm and Tracey exemplify the

new type. Their specialised capabilities are immensely beyond
what would have been expected of them twenty years ago, their
non-specialised capabilities scarcely existent in relation to what
would have been required of them then. Neither of them can, for
instance, lay a hedge, even where there are hedges to lay. Nor
can I, though I know a little of what that job consists.

As a spectator of these changes, I am not alone. There are
millions of us, in one way or another anxious for the well-being
of our countryside. In presuming to speak for any of them, I do
so from the positions of weakness, and of strength, of those who
have no income from the land, nor the aim of producing harvests
at prices which the nation can afford.

We who are thus detached are not for that reason uncon-
cerned. Though not dependent on it, I live on the land because
I could not live (in the full sense) anywhere else; experience
having proved mere existence in a town to be difficult. The land
is my native element. Its separation from towns, or even from
the traffic routes which intersect it, is more distinct to me than
the separation which the Channel constitutes between our
countryside and that of rural France. This does not imply anathema towards towns, or to the people in them. Many of these
are at heart country people too, less fortunate than I, compelled
by occupational necessity to live in surroundings not their
choice.

Similarly, many townsfolk live in the country, but never become of the country. Nor are those who work on the land necessarily countryfolk in essence. One does not become the salt of
the earth merely by living in a village. Not all farmers are inten-
tional cultivators, or conservers of the soil; some, perhaps an
increasing proportion nowadays, are manufacturers by intent,
their eyes on the profits to the exclusion of the processes, max-
imising present output, regarding tomorrow as another day for
somebody else to sort out. I do not rend my garments over this.
Human nature was ever thus, probably always will be. Farming
is an art of the possible, no less than anything else. But facts
should be recognised by those who are like me in feeling the land
in their blood, and who hear the call of it as sailors hear the call

of the sea. The facts bring us no mood of optimism in assessing the prospects of that ancient institution, the good British hedge.

Some hedges are as historic as the most ancient churches of their parishes, and equally entitled to be scheduled as monuments. Some have developed from the deer-leaps of the Normans, ingenious drop-fences which permitted the local magnate's deer to clear his boundary and feed off the villeins' crops when the demesne was browsed bare, and then to jump back. Others are nearly as old, their fruitfulness proportionate to the centuries of their existence. Thanks to the cupidity of an invading Frenchman, I can stock my household each year with sloe, bullace, crabs, wild plum, blackberries, hazel nuts and elderberries without walking a furlong. Hedges accumulate riches as time passes.

Most hedges, however, date only from the enclosures of the eighteenth and nineteenth century. They were planted for two reasons, the second of which is often forgotten, to divide field from field so that the land could be managed in fertile rotations previously impossible, and to provide windbreaks. These prevent the top-soil blowing from tillage in dry Springtime gales, and give warmth and shelter to livestock in Winter when down to pasture.

They also confer two fringe benefits, mention of which may sound frivolous to manufacturer-farmers but are highly valued by those who wish the countryside to be something better than a nationwide factory floor. They can be jumped-over by foxhunters, and they provide immense acreages of cover and nesting places for wild life of all kinds of which game birds are a minority, though an important one. Even now this area is greater than that occupied by motorways. It is a comforting realization, possibly the only such, that the face of Britain in its symmetry of forest, coppice, hedgerow and open ground is safe so long as sporting rights maintain their present value, and hence their stabilising influence on the care of landscapes.

Equally important, though less self-evident, is their stabilising influence on wild life. All creatures need light, air, security and space. Large woodlands are not the thickly populated habitats that some people assume. Their edges will be full of life, their close-grown centres less so, if not wholly empty. Those who, seeing a forest from its periphery, assume its birds, animals and insects to be evenly distributed give themselves a false impression. But a hedge is all edge and no centre. Natural development of undergrowth as well as main stems give it a width of four or five yards at ground level, a perfect stronghold for natural species of all kinds smaller than fallow deer. But to earn their place in the scheme of things, hedges must fulfill their primary purpose. If they are to divide, they must be impenetrable.

To keep the hedges stock proof is a major Winter work. When manpower was plentiful on the land hedges were strengthened by human skill each fifteen years or so. Every yard was trimmed out and, with a skill now almost lost, reinforced until it presented an obstacle of Colditz strength to the most bloody-minded bullock. It was hard work for weatherproof men who knew the component plants, how all would grow, and how to impose their will upon them. Using the forces of Nature in years still to come, farm hands who would have guffawed at being called artists wove together the foundation plants over thousands of miles of hedge varying from the pliant hazel of the chalk counties to stiff thorns on strong Midland soils.

All done in the open Winter scene, before the sap began to rise, it was hard work as well as skilled. Twenty-two yards was a man's stint for a day, and it needed a real man to do it. Was this how the length of a cricket pitch was decided, by the strong-armed yokels of Hampshire and Sussex? There are less likely explanations. Cutting and laying, pleaching, and stake-and-bound were the techniques, hook and glove the tools. Growths that had gone away upright in mid-hedge were nicked by a billhook, the blow so precisely weighted that it split the trunk while leaving the bark and the sap-carrying cambium layer intact on what was to be the under-side. A man who eyed his stint in the morning would decide within five minutes which growths would go and which would stay, which intertwine with others. Then he would take all day to carry it out.

Such, for weeks, was the life of a farm labour force after autumn ploughing was done, Spring seeding not begun. Out in

the grey and vigorous weather a man could be alone; needed to be, with all his mind on so detailed a job. In school holidays I and others like me helped at fatigue-man level, as with lambing. We went from hedger to hedger, raking and pitching the brashings, then firing them and seeing the blue smoke trails torn away, acrid as fresh pepper on the winter wind. Sometimes the rhythmic smack of boetel on stake would cease, a great silver turnip watch come out, and snap-time be declared. We would use the upwind heat of the fire to give us comfort while we ate.

No matter who was my companion, and I helped out for dozens long ago and far away, the ritual was always the same. We walked back to the spot in the cleared ditch where collie dog or terrier lay out of the wind, guarding a stowed bicycle, a waterproof, a lidded blue-enamelled can, and a snap-tin. The dog would come with us, back to the fire. I would open my piece, eager to see what it might be, but there would be no mystery about his master's. A bacon sandwich, chunk of cheese and an onion was the iron rule. So was cold tea from the enamelled can. Vacuum flasks were for gentry; hot tea, presumably, for women at that hour; men at snap-time would as soon have drunk hot beer; always cold tea for those who were taking their spell.

Such men on their own saw much, even with their mind on their work – where the hunt went, what the gipsies did, where a new rabbit bury had been opened and ferrets could do some good. Metaphorically and actually they told me the time of day, when I was a lad about the place. For half an hour, then back to the hedge, a return always signalled across the acres by half-a-dozen boetel smacks in case the guv'nor was within earshot. Hours later the day died slowly as the work crept up to its destined twenty-two yards, the wind hardened, rooks flew over, and a strong, fit man would look at his handiwork (knowing that he would be fated to watch its future as the next fifteen years passed their verdict), and he would know that he was tired. John Clare, the Northamptonshire poet who in his day did more than just burn the brashings, had his say on the end of a day's hedging, "So till morrow morning come, bill and mittens lie ye there". The days did not end then for the likes of me. We would go round the stints of two or three other men, raking up in the dusk, then firing the heaps if the wind were safe, leaving scattered pin-points of orange flames leaping behind us as we went home to draw our shillings.

Recollected in tranquillity, that is how it was. It is rarely done that way now, and therein sounds the death knell of hedges. Whatever the rights and wrongs may be in human terms, the facts remain. Those long tasks, and the men to perform them, cannot be paid for now. Instead of men who went to the root of the matter and saw through it into years to come, the trimming machine must do the job. It looks pretty for a time. But a trimming machine cannot nick and pleach, nor put in stakes to close a gap until strengthening growth can block it. It can take off what is not wanted. But it can create nothing.

The essence of a well-laid hedge was that its natural vertical growth was redirected laterally. Each shrub and bush connected with the next, and the intertwined limbs, strengthening each year, grew tighter and more compact. A hedge was in fact a mesh, not just a row of plants. Neat though a trimmer makes a hedge at first, if viewed from a distance, each component bush is left to grow vertically, so weak places develop between them, and soon a man can barge his way through (watch the beaters on shooting days). Where a man can pass, beasts can do likewise, widening each modest gap until it would admit a hippopotamus. So strands of barbed wire are run lengthways through the hedge to give it the "body" it has come to lack, and a hunt jump is built at a corner to give a communal line to those on horseback.

That is not the end of the story. Lacking the mutual support of a pleached hedge, the weaker growths die off. Some are grazed or browsed out because the trimmers leave hedges more narrow, lacking the breadth which defended the inner core. Other growths are battered down by wind-thrash where winter gales build up and release their pressure through the developing gaps, widening them each time. What was once a thickset barrier becomes instead a line of decapitated trunks, themselves weakened by repeated cutting down to size, instead of being allowed to mature and strengthen in useful directions.

As a windbreak, its days are by that time done. A well-managed hedge was more efficient in this respect than anything which science has devised. Being a porous screen of twigs and branches, it split the air currents and dispersed them instead of merely deflecting the main blast without reducing its force, as a wall does. The effect is apparent to anybody watching March dust fly away in clouds beyond a dry-stone dike. Because of this, a healthy hedge gives an area of positive warmth on its lee-side which, in severe weather, is as good as a blanket each to outlying beasts, which are connoisseurs of comfortable places in rough weather. The effect on food consumption and meat production is the difference between profit and breaking even.

While sound, hedges perform a further service. Their leaves, ripped off by Autumn gales, are blown in showers on to the furrows a hundred yards downwind, then picked up and taken on another fifty, eventually rotting down to put humus into soil which, in modern practice, seldom gets it in any other way. There is not much plant food in the leaves of a single hedge, but the heart they give to the soil enables chemical fertilisers to work, instead of being washed out by succeeding storms.

Without enough skilled manpower, hedges cannot exist as they did. But necessity is the mother of invention. The necessity that they should do so is indisputable, so my hope that they may be saved by some means yet unknown is not quite dead. What is at stake is not primarily their place in our traditions, or their part in our well-loved scenery. The real loss will be their contribution to the economics of stock-raising and soil culture – to which any farmer or accountant, or even our three-day lambs could testify if the alternatives were compared.

WHEN the wind gets stuck in the North it often stays there for weeks. This northerly blows itself out in ten days, and a south-westerly settles in. It skims up moisture from the Atlantic, and drops it on us in successive storms. The earth evaporates some of it back, and we have soft air again instead of the cutting blast of recent days. Lapwing flocks come back to the hills. With them are fieldfares and redwings which took refuge in village gardens and orchards when times were hard. Now the undercurrent of Spring is flowing. Different voices in different places change the key-note of the days; the nights, too.

Listening to the nights is as sure a way as watching the days to tell how the young year is moving on. Now when darkness falls the owls call to each other and answer off and on for hours, a location-reporting network which spans the downland villages.

The shriek of the barn owl passing soft-winged overhead, the broken moan of the long-ear, the tawny's medley of hoots and yaps and the little owl's scrape, all pierce the darkness until midnight, then die away. The time until dawn is by comparison silent – except that now it is clicketting time for foxes, much helped by moist West weather, and we can hear the sound-track.

The clue is a short, hoarse, almost deferential bark, less a command than a hint. It is easily drowned by the evening's owl-to-owl signal traffic, but dramatically eloquent when heard solo against the silence of the small hours. This is the dog fox out there in the night, nearing at long last the vixen on whom his desires are set, and announcing his approach. She can hardly be called the vixen of his choice, for it is unlikely that he has yet seen her, or she him. But she will be ready, or he would not have known of her existence, and when she realises his presence the world will know it too. The banshee scream of a vixen calling on the developing climax is unforgettable, but not always heard for what it is. Some people confuse it with a barn owl's voice, others with a badger. To me it is unmistakeably more animal than bird, and as feminine as the "woman wailing for her demon lover" in Kubla Khan.

Round this stunningly urgent cry in the night centres the design for living of foxes. They have well-earned their reputation, not confined to Britain but world-wide, of being the cool cats of the countryside, living unseen, coming and going without trace, getting by like the smart operators they are. Latterly a rot has set in, dividing them into elite and drop-outs. Many foxes have become dustbin-rangers, breaking the tradition of their kind like gipsies who live in houses, basing themselves in urban outskirts and even inner cities. There they live unsuspected within yards of man, their presumed enemy. That easy life soon leads to degeneration; like the jackals in the East, flicking among the shadows after dark, seldom seen by day. Those clusters of light on which we looked down from the lambing pen know this all too well. Army camps are magnets for foxes which have abandoned the survival-of-the-fittest discipline of life on open hills, and in field or woodland. Scavenging on the frontiers between the foxes' world and ours blights the vulpine heritage of endurance, cunning and enterprise. By their pelts we can know them; russet-backed, clean white below on the genuine fox of the wild, grey and scruffy, often mangey, on the urban parasite.

Out of towns, as in them, there are more foxes than anybody knows. They come and go undetected, until they give themselves away by killing lambs, fowls or game. Except in snow, they leave no clue when they come and go. Then the single line of footprints, regularly spaced and each in exact line with the one in front and the one behind, is unmistakeable. More people smell

foxes than see them, and it is not necessary to consult a fox-
hound for confirmation. The reek of a fox is as unmistakeable as
its footprints and, if in strength, a certain indication that its
earth is near.

For so outwardly spruce an animal, a fox's home is squalid.
Foxes have none of the fastidiousness of badgers. Comfortless
and insanitary, generally littered with discarded bones and mor-
sels inedible even by a fox, an earth proclaims its presence. The
only precaution which foxes take when choosing a home is its
location. There are places, even in farming Britain, where man
does not go, perhaps cannot get. In finding and exploiting them,
foxes have eyes for country like the Japanese infantry officers
who gave to the world's soldiers the concept of the foxhole.

Foxes make a distinction between temporary lie-ups and permanent dwellings. The former are occupied only so long as convenient, the latter for years on end by one fox after another.
Popular as lie-ups are warm places in kale fields; a dry hummock
in an osier bed where the temperature is generally a degree or
two higher than elsewhere because near water; a snug patch,
with plenty of exits, in brambles impenetrable by man; a hol-
lowed pollard willow (there are plenty such). All can be abandoned in a hurry, and are mainly used by young foxes who have
yet to establish themselves at a permanent address.

An earth for long-term occupation is likely to be on high
ground – perhaps the edge of a hill-top copse, in a hanging gorse
clump, or on a cliff-like face of an abandoned quarry or chalk-
pit. Wherever it is, it will have a view. That eye for country is
constantly exploited. Once, when we had marked a fox to ground
on just such a chalk face near my home, I climbed to it with the
terrier man. Having arrived, I realized what I could not have
imagined, the panoramic view it gives of our village, and the
next, and of the vale in which they lie, as revealing as Dylan
Thomas's vision from Milk Wood. Every house and garden lies
open to view. A cat, dozing on a gate post, can be seen, bird's
eye fashion, half a mile away. I had not then known how many
of my neighbours kept hens. But the fox knew. It was his business. Sitting in the sunset glow, inspecting the world around

him, he could assess the options for his next meal.

There, too, in a special sense, he could take the air, as doubtless many another fox has done while these words are being written. This mild damp Atlantic airstream can bring the most compelling of all messages. The duty to procreate, to keep the chain of life going, dominates all other appetites and instincts. Hunger and hazard are obliterated by it. When a dog fox senses the presence of a waiting vixen, he travels. His journey is part of Nature's insurance against the devitalising effect of in-breeding, and it is the wind that brings desire, adds the miles, stretches the separation which must be traversed.

The capacity of foxes to pick up airborne scent at long range reduces the risk of too local an encounter of mates leading to copulation between blood relations. West winds spread the news far and wide because they are damp. Their vapour picks up the scent of a vixen ready and willing, and holds it, dispersing its enticing message to dog foxes down-wind of her for fifteen miles or so. Picking it up as he surveys his territory at sundown, a suitor ceases to think of the next meal.

He tastes the air with mounting excitement, absorbs more and more of the scent until he is fired by a different hunger. When night falls, and a fox can cross the country without men shouting, sheepdogs chasing him, and all the adverse publicity which attends him in daylight, he responds to what is now irresistible and surrenders himself upwind.

Each mile he puts behind him makes the presence ahead more compelling. Acting as a homing beacon, the scent trail guides him to her; perhaps more than one him; he may have to fight for her. Eventually the spell becomes all-powerful. Her presence is everywhere, she is nowhere. The time for caution, for secretiveness, for silence is past. That husky and apologetic bark, so far removed from the self-declaration of an ardent lover, is nevertheless the fox's version of the universal question, Where do I find you?

The answer that tears the night apart also rips open the sleep of the just. Those who waken to it do not forget it. One of the deep-rooted country fallacies will surely be aired next day.

"Hear the old badger last night? Fair screaming she was." The question is asked at the bar, at the shop, in church, wherever else two or three are gathered together, and the wiseacres often say, "That would be the old sow calling." The truth is otherwise.

The old sow badger, if doing anything in particular this night, would have been ten feet underground producing her cubs – ending the process of mating and birth, not starting it. The life-cycle of badgers, giant but non-bloodthirsty members of the weasel family, includes the phenomenon of delayed implantation. They do not mate in Winter but in Summer, as daylight begins to shorten after the solstice. Preferring to slip through life unseen and unheard, badgers give no visible or audible indication of what has taken place, and little else happens for weeks to come because the new life does not at first develop, but stays dormant. Its growth begins in the semi-hibernation of Winter, only two months before the dark days in which the cubs are born.

Badgers are the countryside's secret people, widely but wrongly considered to be rare. Parliament passed an Act to protect them, in the apparent belief that they are an endangered species. They are, in fact, quite common and have recently bred in such unprotected surroundings as Wimbledon Common and Hampstead Heath – as well as practically everywhere in rural Britain. Most Members of Parliament, of course, are townsmen by nature, over-ready to believe that many forms of life, not excluding themselves, are subject to persecution, and that any species which they do not actually see is for that reason close to being extinct.

Nobody, even in the country, often sees badgers. The fact that an animal weighing as much as a bull terrier dog, and two-and-a-half to three feet long, can live in large numbers but unnoticed not merely in suburban London but among observant country folk is not less remarkable for being true. It is also proof of the harmlessness of these physically formidable creatures. They are immensely strong, their jaws are those of flesh-eaters though they are mainly vegetarian, and their ability to dig into or out of anywhere they wish is as near total as makes no difference. Yet damage by badgers is unusual, and because they are not a nuisance they are normally unnoticed. When a badger turns rogue, the situation is very different. Perhaps taste for young rabbits, woodmice, fledging birds which fall from nests fires the appetite of a badger gastronome. Thereafter no poultry, nor any poultry house, is safe from him.

Late Winter is my badger time. To meet them one must be often in woodland, and as nocturnal as they are. The season of the year gives me the chance. More often than not, one knows a badger is near without seeing it. A heavy rustling in thick growth, some wheezing or snuffling, and in Summer an overpowering sudden smell of musk – that odour which has otherwise died out of the world – are generally the only evidence. But now, with undergrowth killed by frost or battered down by storms, sightings are possible.

A FTER the game seasons end, shooting becomes duty first, sport second. Neighbourhoods form alliances against enemies of farming, the irreducible woodpigeons and the resurgent rabbits. When guns go out against them there are rewards, in a quiet way.

Saturdays are woodpigeon days because the number of guns can then be doubled by calling out farm staffs and those who have the day off from work in towns. The need is for guns tactically placed in all big woods, and one in every shelter-belt and spinney, from noon till dark. Noise, and plenty of it, is wanted. It keeps woodpigeons moving.

In Wessex, Winter flocks of woodpigeons are often thousands strong. They eat out fodder crops, market gardens, and newly-sown corn. An unguarded ten-acre field can be stripped in a morning. For the rest of the year woodpigeons are not over-numerous – not because unerring marksmanship keeps their numbers down, but because the Winter flocks are not natives but temporary immigrants. Hard weather in the North rolls back the nationwide woodpigeon population towards the South, concentrating it as it goes. Wessex is the last stop in the oceanic weather zone before the more extreme continental system begins at the French coast. For three months we are hosts to hungry millions. Some say that the refugees from Scotland and the North are reinforced by influxes from Scandinavia, Germany, Holland and Belgium. We neither know nor care whence they come. Our interest is in saving the crops, to which end dispersion is as good as extermination.

So, posted in a spinney, I can hear gunshots from all around, despite the cost of cartridges. The day is cloudy, blowing stiffly from the West, a wet night looming. I find an ash tree, leafless now, to stand beneath. Ash trees are magnets for woodpigeons. Their open branches give a view all round, so they settle there to preen, and to watch what goes on. When airborne they line their routes from one tall ash to the next. We know these landmarks as "pigeon trees". The art of pigeon shooting depends on placing myself under the flightline of the day, having worked it out by watching the pigeon trees. With the wind as it is and me where I am, facing East because pigeons approach upwind, I should have some overhead.

Two o'clock. My cartridge bag is hanging from a handy branch, my gun loaded, the sky empty, my flask nearly full. I correct the latter; the sloe gin will be eked out, a pull per hour, between now and darkness. The spaniel at my feet sits cheerful, tasting the air. She is a springer. A cocker would have dug a hollow, snuggled into it, and gone to sleep by now, as an old soldier would. Cockers are hard-boiled realists, but springers are always optimists, and what they cannot see they can imagine. Time passes.

Three o'clock. Leaning on the ash bole, I feel the whole tree flex itself against the wind, yielding and recovering against my back as its crown and branches toss. Whole forests must heave like this day in, day out over tree-lifetimes which may last several centuries. The anchorage of trees to earth is an unnoticed wonder of the world.

A spatter of dots swings across the sky to the left. They are woodpigeons half a mile off, and likely to turn my way. At that range I cannot recognise them by appearance, nor need to. Except in museums and laboratories we do not identify birds by their feathers; we know them by what they do, and the way they relate to their surroundings. From their flight formation and speed I know that they have lifted from a field where they fed, and are on their way to a safe perch for the next hour or so.

I bend my eyes on to my boots. At half a mile pigeons probably cannot recognise a man, but when trees are bare they can see the unfamiliar light patch of half an upturned human face – all that is visible under the peak of my cap. I count thirty seconds, then raise my eyes. The pigeons are streaming over, about two dozen of them. Two shots, one down. Anybody else would have had two or more. I had missed, then connected with the choke barrel. The bird falls well out, into some withered rosebay. The spaniel sits tight. She marked the fall, telling me so by keeping her eyes on it and lifting a forepaw. When I give her the word, she is away to fetch it.

She delivers it with distaste, shaking herself as she spits out feathers. I know how she feels. There is something unwholesome about woodpigeons when dead which is at variance with their spirited selves when airborne. This one is in high condition, his plumage a clean mix of pastel blue, pink and white, his neck feathers touched with shining green, smooth with health, unruffled by his instant death in full flight. In an hour he will have faded to drab nonentity, nothing attractive about him, despite the delicious pie that his breast meat will make, despite his kind being very sporting birds – less predictable and often faster than pheasants, partridges or grouse, and flying higher.

Four o'clock. The light softens. Through a cloud gap I see the winter sun go down. So does the sloe gin. More pigeons flash overhead, some of them doing their usual trick of appearing from nowhere and going nowhere, others circle the copse, one or two fall. The sound of others shooting intensifies as roosting time approaches. A circle of ejected cartridge cases surrounds me. Doing a rough count my eye is caught by another eye at ground level, and behind it a snake-like green head. A cock pheasant has footed in, under a fallen branch five yeards away. He is down-wind, but the spaniel knows he is there. She lengthens her neck as she stretches and leans to see more, but is too polite to move. This is the close season, a time to be sniffy about pigeons, but as good a time as any other for decent behaviour towards pheasants.

Five o'clock. More pigeons flight in. I fire a dozen more shots, quickly and with the footwork needed to find clear arcs between trees. The air is sharp with cartridge smoke, twigs are still dropping when the echoes die. The pheasant's eye still meets mine. He has not moved and does not intend to, unless the spaniel forcibly ejects him. Gunshots mean nothing to him. There were no gunshots when the reflexes and thought-processes of his species evolved thirty million years ago. Despite their recent destiny as game, they still have no fear of gunshots. One day, after Spring and Summer, a gunshot will probably be the end of him. But he knows nothing of that now, and if he is killed clean he will know nothing of it then.

33

Other birds come in to roost. Jackdaws in line astern head for the warmth of ivy on some oak boles, prinking blackbirds tuck themselves into a hazel clump, robins and dunnocks pass to secret destinations, ribald starlings flock in some tall branches. All the local birds that we could contribute to Noah's Ark are in procession at day's end, a sight as compelling as if I had never seen it previously. The first raindrops fall. As evening thickens some shooting is still going on, but my conscience tells me that I have made enough noise, and we can now stand down. I break the gun, slip out the cartridges, but wait longer to watch the quiet transition into night as the rain rattles on my waterproof, and bird calls fade into silence.

A roebuck, grey in winter pelage, steps nimbly between the trees, stops in amazement, looks at us eye to eye from fifteen yards, then flashes away in overdrive, the white patch of his backside swerving expertly, like a pony in a bending race. Now, of course, would be the time to see a badger, except for the rain; they will stay warm and dry tonight, living off their fat, of which most badgers have plenty. Only a hare comes by, in no hurry until she sees the spaniel. I load myself with cartridge bag and game bag, check that the now empty flask is in my pocket. We move out on a line which will not disturb the pheasant, and take bearings on the darkened world outside the spinney.

The rain is soughing down now. There is no light to make the sodden furrows gleam. Nothing guides us save the misty outlines of distant woods, and the sound of some homing swain's motorcycle on the main road. The spaniel walks soberly beside me. Perhaps her thoughts are mine. Four hours. A long time to devote to a mere pest, especially so distasteful a pest as woodpigeons. But there have been fringe benefits. We have been together. We have seen things. We have been in peace.

At the house, shooters are coming in from all directions. There is much clumping about, and changing of boots for indoor footwear. Our host has a piece of millboard, with a bulldog clip, in this respect resembling a sergeant-major. He is noting our accomplishments, greeting mine with charitable lack of comment. For the next hour firelight reddens faces which the weather smartened. Tea, plum cake and whisky, a combination excelling all restoratives, go the rounds. So do stories. Somebody claims a one-to-four kills to cartridges ratio. Stock-taking on return home reveals mine as one-to-seventeen. A proud record, if not of marksmanship, then of duty done. Those that miss make just as much noise.

I F I had to spend a calendar month out of Britain (which heaven forbid), and could choose, it would be February. Apart from grey skies, mud, perhaps some snow there would not be much to miss; nothing, indeed, except the first Spring day, and rabbit shooting. The first Spring day, very different from the first day of Spring which is still weeks away, always comes in February, so is unquestionably part of Winter. Fleetingly and not to be repeated, out of the cheerless background there happens a day of jewel-like quality to promise the good things ahead. It is a day out of its season, a day of grace which Winter gives us before relapsing into the harsh obduracy of its normal self.

Today is that day, as blind men know as well as any. What reveals Spring in the midst of Winter is the most evocative of all the senses, smell. The visible signs are inconclusive; it cannot be said of Spring that we know it when we see it, only when we breathe it. The sky can be cloudless in Winter; there may even be warm days. The sun shines then as bright as at any time, if seldom. But these are not Spring days. The essence of Spring is given out on the air waves by the soil and the plants which grow in it.

There is nothing blatant about it, like the audible transition in the tropical East when monsoon ends the dry weather. There, after the deluge and the thunder crash, the bamboo brakes creak in the calm that follows, creaking with the friction of new growth bursting from their sheaths. Here, the signs of life revived are more subtle; so subtle that at first they pass their message unaware. Receiving it, we stand still to savour it again; then analyse whence it comes. By some lucky combination of humidity, temperature, barometric pressure, and windlessness we catch fresh breath from the earth, and the fragrance of young leaf. At ground level there is just enough of it to enliven the air; the first celandine and coltsfoot at hedge-root; wood anemone and dog's mercury on forest floors. Head high, catkins are open on willows and hazel. The unfelt touch of the year's first pollen impregnating the air is enough to make us suddenly aware, turning our thoughts towards the build-up which leads to the richness of Summer.

That this heavenly day will pass, like all the others, is of no consequence. Like the rainbow, it is a pledge, so vivid that we do not doubt it will be honoured. We can wait, being reminded of what is worth waiting for.

Meanwhile on days less glorious, rabbits ascend the rural agenda. Since myxomatosis nearly made them extinct thirty years ago, their recovery has been slow, but is a fact. Now in particular, when barrenness reveals all, the woods and headlands are street maps of the rabbit community's daily round. Where tree roots hold the soil together, and guarantee a sound roof, the re-established race of rabbits are tunnelling in as they did in days of yore. Even an ash or hazel stole gives security enough, and we can respond with a qualified welcome. In any plantation past sapling stage, rabbits cause little harm, and the scene is more attractive for their presence. Their havoc is done in the fields around. Twenty-yard strips of winter corn, eaten-off short at the edge of woods tell the story.

So does the view from a train. Few vantage points are as good as a railway carriage window for seeing wild life. Despite their noise, vibration and general disturbance, trains themselves become accepted by animals and birds as normal components of their background. Railway tracks, unlike major roads, lie through unspoiled countryside. Rail travellers, with no need to look where they are going, and with an elevated view from every embankment, can see without distraction all that goes on. The altered status of the rabbit from endangered species to resurgent pest is therefore obvious. Instead of the rare sighting, too often of a stricken myxomatosis sufferer hobbling along with only a narrow lead over its approaching death, brisk upstanding healthy rabbits are again out and about over most of farming Britain, especially in February. Against the shortened growth of grass and crop, they show themselves boldly beside woods and hedges when they feed in the afternoon sunshine.

There is no absolute about modern rabbits. A species with such survival potential, not to mention population dynamics, had to become adaptable. He who lives alongside rabbits, as we in the country are fated to do, soon sees examples of this. One is in their appearance. In very few generations, rabbits' colouration changes to tone with their locality. Our Wessex rabbits are grey, not the hodden grey of Patrick Chalmers's verses (which were doubtless true of rabbits on the Scottish Border), but almost steel grey. This matches the dusty, chalk-impregnated downland soil. Where the land is loam or clay, rabbits are a clean bright brown, near to the colour of a chestnut horse.

These colours are not related to similar contrasts in rabbit life patterns, though these also vary. As with foxes, recent events have divided rabbits into two communities. When myxomatosis virus was introduced and spread among the grossly excessive rabbit population of the early post-War years (numbers having expanded while the young men of the rural population were in the Forces or busy on essential work) fleas transmitted it from rabbit to rabbit. Such vectoring by a parasite is characteristic of fatal diseases in all species, including our own, as witness bubonic plague and typhus. Therefore concentrated rabbit communities were more vulnerable than isolated families.

Burrows became hotbeds of infection. There, rabbits lived closely together and flea-swapping was inevitable. The underground-based rabbit population was virtually wiped out by 1960. But a minority of rabbits have always lived on the surface, a life-style known as "sitting out". Their "seats" are couching places in the ground where overgrowth protects them from rain, between tussocks of coarse grass, under dead bracken, beneath brambles or heather. These rabbits lead relatively solitary lives, going below only to breed. Then the kindling doe digs a blind tunnel, known as a "stop", in which the young are born, and which they leave when old enough to fend for themselves. Being less exposed to fleas carrying the infection, surface-dwelling rabbits had a correspondingly lower myxomatosis death-rate. From being a historic minority, they are now a majority, perhaps only temporarily.

The consequences for their human neighbours are all too apparent. Rabbits always damage cultivated crops, whether broad acres or cottage gardens. But open air rabbits, being more mobile, enterprising and alert than the burrow dwellers, are proportionately less easy to deter, exclude, or kill. A generation of gardeners has grown up to whom rabbits have hitherto been no serious problem. Now they are learning the truth about them. One is that although the difficulty of keeping rabbits out of a garden is considerable, even for those who can afford the necessary wire netting, it is less tantalising than the problem of persuading a rabbit to leave, or ending its existence, when once it is inside. The charisma which the rabbit continues to hold for most of us long after it has ceased to be the bunny of our childhood, fades rapidly when even the most benevolent householder finds himself host to an unwanted rabbit. He suspects on sound grounds that there will soon be more than one.

Farmers must plan counter-measures far enough in advance to prevent rabbits becoming a menace. So unofficial neighbourhood vigilantes, similar to the anti-pigeon networks, come into being. Most of the Government supported Rabbit Clearance Societies are fading memories now, the rabbits (as usual) having won.

The burrow-dwellers can be tackled, with local success assured, either by ferrets or by gassing, the latter being a euphemism for the toxic suffocation so strangely advocated by animal protection societies. The people behind these organisations seldom think straight. We read of them advocating shooting and poison (including gas) as "humane" methods for the destruction of foxes but to stigmatise poison (including gas) as inhumane when used against badgers. And the shooting which they recommend for foxes becomes "cruel" when it is pheasants which are shot. They talk so much nonsense that I wonder why they bother to talk at all. Perhaps they do so from an undefiled spirit of busybodyism.

The skills and mysteries of ferreting have passed me by since boyhood, that period in life when, in the country, it is impossible not to possess a ferret. I have learned that if encountered in action, ferreters are best left alone. Like people preparing for examinations or composing symphonies, total silence is their pre-requisite. There are times when crowbar and spade are plied with sweating, grunting energy but they are separated by longer and suspense-laden interludes when, literally, all present have their ears to the ground, following the progress of the ferrets amid the tunnels and galleries deep in the earth. With all exits blocked by nets, developments come in their own good time, and the repute of a dutiful, enterprising and successful ferret stands high for miles around.

Ferrets, the sinuous and bloodthirsty "pugs" of the country-man, have never been near my heart since my twelfth year when one of the only three I ever possessed bit through my hand in a moment of pique. Since then I have been impressed by the devotion to them of many good secretive, if gruff countrymen – few of whom have been total abstainers. And I have been equally impressed at the other devotion which ferrets elicit from small girls who coo over them, stroke and pet them, wearing round their necks like mufflers creatures such as that which did not scruple to clench its teeth with my palm between them.

With that memory I am far from surprised that rabbits should decide to make a prompt exit on finding ferrets infiltrating their subterranean homes. The reception planned for them on the surface means that this is the last decision most of them ever make. It is impossible not to feel a momentary surge of pro-rabbit sentiment at this realization. And yet, despite the knowledge that those which escape are few, I would rather take my chance with the bloodthirsty enemy below and the odds against me above than the alternative. That is to crouch helpless, with every exit blocked and airtight, while gas, the acrid, corrosive, creeping death, invades my breath and eventually kills me. Being underground, hence invisible, that form of slow death is easily forgotten by those preferring not to think about it. But one of the three, the ferrets' teeth, the man-placed net, or gas is inflicted on thousands of burrow rabbits every day of the main killing season in the lean weeks when the growth is down and before other farm work becomes demanding. Perhaps, after all, the ferrets' teeth are the most merciful.

None of these things happen to sitting-out rabbits. They have more manœuvrability, are less easily located, and learn the skills of survival. They know that the greatest of these is to lie low. Most of their seats are made where a human foot will never fall. If it does, a seated rabbit lies so tight that the passing boot must be within a foot or so to make him bolt. A yard is a long way to an outlying rabbit, unless the intruder stops. Then a rabbit may lose its nerve and bolt. Otherwise they are wise enough to know that while continued immobility means they are undetected, more often than not, a pause means that they have been seen, or are being sought. Either way, a man by himself poses little threat. The initiative is with the rabbit, the odds are on him, and he generally lands them.

So I volunteer my services, my spaniels and my gun, to clear rabbits from twenty-five acres of bracken banks and tussocks overlaid by dead bramble beside a brook. This is not ground where rabbits burrow. The soil is too poor; thin stuff, it does not support tree growth nor is it weatherproof overhead. Choosing their spots, rabbits lying out are safer and more comfortable. Two of us walk the ground slowly upwind behind the dogs.

Spaniels are the commando soldiers among gundogs. Quick witted, quick moving, adaptable, determined, unstoppable at getting under, over, or through obstacles, and always optimistic, they bring their noses, brains and tails to bear on problems which our eyes cannot solve. They not only find rabbits which we would never see, and flush them out of cover into the open where a shot is possible, but they give a running commentary too. The ever-moving spaniel tail wags at differing tempo according to what its nose is telling it, constituting its own morse code which a man can learn to read.

A low-held tail vibrating narrowly means, "I have hopes"; a broader wag, "positive prospect here"; increasingly urgent action, "target ahead"; a raising of the tail towards spine-level, "stand by for action". In addition a well-trained spaniel, working for a man it trusts, repeatedly glances back at him as the scent of quarry strengthens, checking his position to ensure that the rabbit bolts towards the gun and not away from it, nor out of range. When the understanding is complete, a dog learns to catch the man's eye in regular communication, while the man learns how to take its hints, interpreting all the signs so that when the rabbit is flushed it comes as no surprise and a safe, clean-killing shot is possible.

Once the previously invisible rabbit moves, the dog must stop instantly. Unless it does so, the shooter is distracted from his shot, and the dog itself may be in danger. At that moment the dog may have been hunting for several minutes in an area permeated by the scent of a rabbit, knowing it is present but unable to locate it. The spaniel's expectancy mounts, lifting its excitement to high pitch. To "drop" motionless at the moment of fulfilment is an act of high discipline. I think my spaniels know this as well as I do, and would think me a churl if I forgot their well-earned word of praise. Certainly the look in their eyes if I then miss the rabbit – more sorrow than anger, but not a lot between them – reflects the wholeheartedness of their sense of partnership.

Two spaniels responsive to every command, working together, hunting out over the ground and under the brambles, forcing their way, lifting the dead growth on their shoulders, twisting in and out in an unflagging rhythm and a systematic pattern, are exhilarating to follow, and two dogs plus two men a perfect team. Rabbits being ground game, the risk of accident is never higher. A larger party multiplies the risk.

Our twenty-five acres occupy an action-packed afternoon, until the sun sets red in a mist which will turn to frost. One thing is certain. When we all take our places in the Land Rover to drive home to tea, no rabbits remain where we have worked so intently. Eleven are in the bag. Another three have gone elsewhere, I having missed them.

My companion of the day would not have done so. The skill of rabbit shooting, so different from that of game-shooting, faded for years with the rabbit itself but is now recovering, and he does not fail. It is best to be a tall man, so gaining better visibility and a high-angled shot. Most essential of all is to be rabbit-wise, to predict subconsciously the line that each will choose through the changing lie of the land, and so be able to take a safe, unhurried shot and see the flash of white belly as the rabbit, dead in its stride, rolls over with the force of its own momentum. Then the spaniel has more to do.

At its own level, eyes about eighteen inches above the ground, its view obstructed by intervening growth, it can know little of what has happened. It had a split second glimpse of the rabbit going away, no more. It heard the shot. The shooter knows where the rabbit was killed, but not where it is now. The dog

does not know either. A running rabbit can roll a long way if the ground is sloping, almost certainly finishing hidden by vegetation. Finding it is work for a nose, not eyes.

So the spaniel which found the rabbit, and therefore has prior rights to it as *his* rabbit, is sent to retrieve. He uses the only knowledge he has, its line of departure. Picking up the foot scent, he tracks it to the point where the shot's impact created a blood scent. There, experience has taught him, will be an abrupt change of direction, and rabbits do not generally roll uphill. Seconds later he will have found the rabbit, and delivered it into the hand of him who held the gun.

If it is my hand, then the consummation, not the rabbit, is my reward. We did it together. Because of that joint achievement, recognition of an objective fulfilled unites us. We have found and brought to hand a wild creature which, for one reason or another, was a necessary operation. This rising to the occasion against the wild, is the spirit of sport. The killing alone, if nothing else were involved, would be merely a disagreeable task. Our small triumphs do not blind me to a minor mystery. Had I not carried a gun, as would happen if I were working a dog for somebody else, many a spaniel would not have retrieved to me, but to the shooter. Gundogs inherit an inexplicable respect for firearms, endowing them with high prestige, recent though they are as a formative influence in their evolution. When we say that a dog "works to the gun", we mean just that.

"I don't know how you can bear to kill them," said a lady of the village one evening as I walked home carrying two rabbits from the edge of a harvest field. She had led a sheltered life since the second World War removed her husband, rising to senior status in a bank, reading widely, organising local concerts. I could not explain to her. What she thought of me as we went our ways I could not know. It did not matter. Within a year she telephoned, asking me to drop in for a drink; and bring my gun. She had joined a majority unsuspected by her, those indignant at having one of the charming little creatures in the garden, many fewer seedlings, and total failure in all attempts to usher it out.

43

March, that young lion, comes roaring in with traditional virility, putting a stop to rabbit shooting. In high winds even the hardened sitters-out move into woodlands. Good dogs can still find them there, but the cover is too tall and thick to give much chance of a shot. So I stay at home, listen to the wind, and watch its effects.

THE four winds have differing accents when heard from my house, and no doubt from many others. The lie of the land, the natural and man-made surroundings give each wind a strictly local character. Here an easterly such as this is deflected upwards by a shoulder of downland. So we hear it whistling over, high in the sky, without the thrashing of tree-tops as an accompaniment. A northerly comes in across the village and along the face of the down, not over it. So we hear the tree noises rather than the wind itself. These are dry winds, more likely in Winter to bring snow than rain. Downpours come from the south-west. Then our house is the first of the village in their track, and they strike us in full fury, rain lashing against windows and wind shaking the whole building. From the comfort of bed on stormy nights we eavesdrop on the weather outside, and seldom draw wrong conclusions.

When we are lucky, March is a turning point. The hard dry breath of the North and East does nothing to make us warm or comfortable. On the contrary, it is the year's severest weather. But it dries the land. Fanning away the top moisture, and that which follows it upwards by capillary attraction, it speeds the plough and its attendant tackles. This year, with a wet and early Winter behind us, every farmer is waiting for the drying-out. Suddenly the whole countryside roars with engines. Tractors criss-cross the landscape drawing furrows, making tilths, drilling seed, rolling, spreading fertilisers, clanking and rattling as they turn.

These industrial reverberations, as much as the wind the authentic voice of March, are continuous for hours. They stop briefly at mid-day when every implement for miles is parked while its driver eats his lunch. Then the all-round roar starts again, and continues until dusk. Even then some of the farms work on by headlights into the night. The levelling beams of sunset shine through a drifting mist, county-wide, the precious March dust that was once valued metaphorically at a guinea a peck. It was a parabolic way of saying that seed sown into dry, new-tilled soil will germinate readily when the next rain falls and, off to a good start, is heading for a profitable crop.

This explosive energy whereby the land is pulverised into productivity, as distinct from the old concept of being wooed, is the voice of modern March. "Everything's rush and tear," the farmers say. They are right. There will be nothing like it until harvest, and there is a limit to how much harvest can be hurried. On well-dried, empty land there is no such limit at tilling time, so I head for steep downsides, which even power-farming cannot cultivate, in search of peaceful miles.

Already there are violets underfoot, the "stinking violets" of the old-time foxhunters who found in them not an obstruction to the scenting power of hounds, but a reminder that the bleak intimation, To Finish the Season, would soon be added to the meet cards. Another transformation is proving wonderfully swift, this time from Winter into Spring.

Spring begins in small particles, hardly bigger than raindrops. Regretting having trodden on a violet, I find it virtually impossible not to tread on many more. The turf here is old, perhaps primeval. The myriad plants that compose it may be the direct vegetative descendants *in situ* of some that were bent by a Viking heel. It has woven its own design of grasses, herbs, and flowers which in their turn have knit themselves together into a fabric of small worlds to which Spring comes when each is ready.

Wherever some declevity, perhaps only an inch deep, faces the sunshine, misses the frost and is out of the wind, there a violet flowers. That modest, delicate bloom, unassisted by the store-house of a bulb, waits in the wings to be first in taking the stage, first to proclaim the end of each year's austerity. How odd that foxhunters should ever have reviled violets, on whatever pretext, especially as traditionalists among them will be wearing corn-flowers identical in hue only a few weeks hence as a close-season badge of their allegiance.

Soon that old turf will be bright with other flowers. First the primrose, then the cowslip, and in high Summer ox-eye daisies which bloom wherever the land is steep. Nearby, there will be others. In the woods bluebells and purslane, ragged robin and lords and ladies, the forbidden foxglove and, in hedgerow shade, bachelor's button and cranesbills; underfoot, small beauties like restharrow and pheasants' eye. I can remember the days of innocence when children picked them as part of their joy in life. Now they are sentenced to adult disapproval and a guilt complex for giving themselves that pleasure. By our own folly, as well as force of circumstances, we have separated our own generation from the good earth, and its flowers are not for us to pick.

A few miles are now behind, and still a few more ahead. The track, one that the Romans used so probably here before them, lies along a contour and leads on to a notch in the sky-line. Perhaps it was along this track that our long distant forerunners, by who-knows-what ingenuity and who-knows-why human sweat, with a diligence that must have exceeded their short life spans, inched the monoliths that now compose Stonehenge. My less arduous journey takes me away from that place of mystery, over the next escarpment, past the lambing pen, and into the valley where the farmhouse stands. There Tracey will be giving intensive care to the final batch of marginal cases before leaving for her next job. It is a last chance to wish her well.

The new view from the notch in the hills shows ancient and modern in perpetual conflict. Its permanent visible features date anywhere between the last Ice Age and the second millenium BC. With the possible exception of a church or two, nothing added later looks anywhere near permanent, or even long-term. The farmhouses and cottages, being in the main chalk cob and

thatch, will either be bulldozed or dissolve in the everlasting
Wessex rain before many more centuries have passed. Our own
generation's contribution, metal grain silos mainly in trios, are
scheduled as temporary structures. Between the primeval and
the present, there is not much.

At the notch the track drops steeply into the next valley.
Below is a sight which I see only at intervals of years, always
thinking that it may be for the last time. Where the downside
meets level land, smoke is rising. Two tents, two hovels and a
vardo are grouped where a junction of track and lane encloses
half an acre of rough ground. Gipsies have camped there time
and again across the years. As Masefield saw in *The Everlasting
Mercy*,

> Three ribbed horses wrenching grass,
> Three wild boys to see me pass,
> And one old woman by the fire,
> Hulking a rabbit warm from wire.

But I do not pass. The old woman stands up when I ask where
her menfolk are. She looks at me levelly and silently for what
would be a long time anywhere else, but gipsies do not hurry
speech. She dries her hands carefully on a piece of sacking. She
is as weathered and wind-twisted as the blackthorns behind her,
and has no teeth. At last she answers.

"What use would I have with men, gentleman?" She laughs.
"See me, and how old I am."

"I am going to the farm," I said. "Perhaps I shall see your
men there."

"I know nothing of the farm, nothing of men. Good day,
gentleman."

"Good day, mother."

The brief encounter, so short and stark, produces a strange
intimacy. Never having seen each other previously we meet, we
part, the barrier between us unpenetrated, yet as if we had
known each other all our lives. She would tell me nothing; to
her, all information is a secret, her property. George Borrow

47

would have recognised the phrases, and the cadences. There are people who live contemporary with nuclear energy, silicon chips, hydrogen bombs and space travel, but for whom nothing changes that is real to them. These are they.

The boys, whom I had not heard move, are gone when I turn away. Round one of the hovels hens are foraging, hens which are worth a second look. A long dog peeps from the door of the other. The vardo, that ancient, hooped-back, ornamental, painted wagon which is home and shrine to travelling people, has its door open. Without committing the solecism of appearing to look, I steal a glance in passing, just as a vote of confidence. Camp ends at the four-step shelf-ladder which leads up to the entrance. In the dim interior reflected light gives glimpses of polished wood, cupboards with brass handles, a gleaming copper kettle, neatness and order; a single stride can take in no more before it carries me beyond the zone of other folks' privacy.

The travelling people have been an endangered species for years, generations perhaps. Like the foxes, men's hands are against them. Like the foxes, many of them have taken to life in towns, or at least in houses. But still, for a few like these, only the road is home. The road is not necessarily metalled or paved or recognisable or predictable; it is simply where they want to go. To move on is in their blood. To live in one place, even in wealth, would be prison. They must put the miles behind them, and have more miles ahead. If they are obsolescent in our modern scheme of things, so too their outmoded freedoms and their peace are foreign to the tyranny by organisation to which most folk must now submit – that peace which is more precious to them because it is defended by the blank wall of non-communication with all who would conform them out of it.

They are becoming fewer. But for those that remain, travelling is what life is, instead of settling to some gainful occupation like car-breaking or totting. And while a single vardo still sways and bumps along the hidden tracks of Britain, they keep alive the right to liberty on their terms.

There is no movement at the entrance to the farm buildings, nor has there been any for some time. Hens, these too worthy

of a second look, are dusting under some elders and guinea fowls pick grit. From somewhere, which proves to be a bull pen temporarily unoccupied by a bull, comes the sound of voices. I enter, with the self-satisfaction of one whose supposition has proved correct. Three men are inside, the farmer and two strangers, dark, slim men, wind-tanned, with side-whiskers linking ears to chin. They wear blue suits which, though neat, sit oddly on them. The atmosphere is high level diplomacy, expressing cordial relations.

This farmer values friendship, including that of the travelling people. Not every year, but most, a vardo comes. When it does, his Land Rover grinds past, and something falls from the passenger door; half a sack of oat tailings, a bag of swedes, a bale of hay. He neither halts nor speaks. To do a good turn and then call attention to it is self-praise to travelling people, hence bad manners. Similarly, to give thanks would seem to them ostentatious, pushing as it were. There are other ways. Pheasants will be unpoached, poultry populations not reduced, a few words will reach a few ears, and a few instances of bad luck will not occur. In the fullness of time a good turn can always be repaid. As now.

This farmer is a countryman. Not all are, though farmers are occupationally committed to living in the country. Domicile does not mean commitment, regard for the future, a sense of belonging, without all of which the word countryman is a misnomer. This man's thinking goes beyond making his pile and getting out. True, he is successful. He has the modern hallmark of the solvent agriculturist, a cabin cruiser in his barn all winter. But he has other assets which are far from modern hallmarks.

"Come in, and get that door shut before this lot fly out," he says.

He and his visitors are regarding a duckwing gamecock and two pile hens (pile is a feather pattern in game fowl). Their like had caused my second glances beside the vardo, and at the farm gate. The cock steps imperiously round the bare floor, an arrogant fellow, a little over-dressed to my taste, his hackles and breechings just a little fulsome. But he is light on his feet, with that contempt for the world around him which bespeaks a fighter's pride.

"That one could win the Oxford, gentleman," says one of the dark faced men. That old-time salutation is no longer used in the singular by any but gipsies.

Oxford was by tradition the place for the annual show of Old English game cocks, the fighting families which have been kept in being since mains were made illegal in 1849. Whatever the shortcomings of the human element in cock fighting, there was nobility in the cocks. A duckwing would be a novelty for this farmer. His stud of black-breasted reds have been in his family for 135 years, handed down father to son from his Cumbrian ancestors since prohibition, and now domiciled in this wide yard, flanked by byres and shelters, smelling of sweet straw, on the wide Wessex plain.

"Friends, would you think of selling him," the farmer asks.

"We would not sell him, gentleman. We give him to you, with the clockers." The demure little hens are content. They have found grit in a corner.

There are handshakes, but still no thanks. All present know that this does not end the matter; with travellers, for good or ill, there is no such thing as an end to anything. Only interruptions.

The farmer's wife arrives with drinks, cut-glass decanters and glasses on a silver tray. The dark men's eyes caress the tray fully

and lovingly for one-tenth of a second each. In other circumstances, it could be melted down inside twenty minutes. Cut glass does not impress them, they might be daily users of it. Perhaps they are. The inside of a vardo can contain anything.

We leave the bull-pen and the duckwing cock with his two dames, and stand in the sunlit yard. Internally measured, it is a forty-yard square. On our side of it is a black-breasted cock with his jet harem, on the other side, a second cock similarly attended. There is another in the foldyard, the farmer says, two more at steadings out on the hills, and the gamekeeper always walks a stag for him. That is enough to keep the line alive. He will settle the duckwing in the walled garden.

The dark men praise the cocks with slow courtesy. They decline further drinks. Strong drink, to them, is a pleasure too rare to be devalued by repetition. Hospitality, however, is to be acknowledged, and they thank the farmer's wife, addressing her as "lady". Then they leave, two muscular, civil-suited figures with rakish hats, heading back to the matriarch who denied knowledge of them. But not, I think, out of my life. Somewhere, by a predestined chance, we shall meet again. Perhaps on a Scottish braeside, which they will have reached moving mainly at night on lanes and byways the length of Britain, dodging main roads. Men will call them tinkers there.

"About twenty pound, wouldn't you say, that duckwing cock," mused the farmer, watching them go. "I'll make it right with them. I'll think of something. I'll have to; before they do."

With so much fighting heritage free in so confined a space, I wonder that all survive. Most of the time, the farmer says, they stay in their own territories. Each of the first two cocks is king on his own side of the yard, a trespasser on the other. If in Spring time, when the old Adam gets into him, one of them trespasses, the local potentate will evict him – in his version of a civilised fashion, using only so much force as is necessary to maintain his rights. The interloper, if stoutly resisted, does not fight to a finish, retreating when the prospect of easy victory fades. The other, after a successful defence, does not follow up to emphasise the defeat he has inflicted. To re-establish the *status quo* is good enough in Nature, retribution not a factor. And an intruder, once successfully resisted, does not intrude again. Only if denied the option of retreat would they fight it out to the end.

There seems to be a lesson here for *homo sapiens*. It is not the only one. This balance of power would cease to exist if the farmer allowed too many males to be in the yard. Then territories would become too small. The right of defence would be replaced by the need for conquest to obtain acceptable living space, as the human race has been driven to do. Then there would be fights to the death. It is not material sufficiency which establishes peace and harmony; there is no lack of food and water, roosts and dusting places in a farmyard. What every creature needs is room to be alone. An affluent society is not a contented society without space, as modern human life demonstrates.

Tracey arrives, with her blend of the self-deprecatory and the self-pleased. She is pleased also with her marginals. She talks idiomatically about her next pad. If I was the chap on the oil rig, I would get moving.

After lunch I do get moving, on my road-less homeward seven miles across the downs. Soon I am again passing the travellers' camp. This time there is no sign of life, no smoke, no movement, no sound. The vardo is closed, the tents brailed, the hovels secretive. Yet I know that I am seen. Somewhere, near or far, eyes are on me, and I can feel that this is so; we all know when we are being watched. The forewarning is easily activated in humanity because bred into us by our remote ancestors who, in a then hostile world, needed every awareness in fulfilling Nature's basic law to survive and beget. Remnants of our early warning systems have not deserted us yet.

THE sun is behind me now. Without its highlight to dazzle
down the view ahead, sapping the colour out of the land, the
year's progress can be seen. The monochromes of Winter are
superceded now, replaced by the brightening hues of Spring –
new green in the grass, a faint haze given to distant woods by
the opening of millions of buds, less starkness everywhere.

Two hares, boxing on a skyline, are russet coated instead of
winter grey, so soon does the touch of sun on their backs produce
the well-being that makes the change. This amiable, slightly
ridiculous display, arousing doubts about the sanity of hares in
March, seems to be a virility symbol rather than a matter of
trespass. I cannot see the lady in the case, but she will not be
far away. Perhaps she is beyond the hill, having a quiet nibble,
or sun-bathing while her hopeful squires dispute their order of
priority. If she hopes for a quick settlement she is an optimist.
Hares are not good at making up their minds, or at reaching
conclusions of any kind.

In these contests the jacks are better at pulling their punches
than at landing them, perhaps anxious lest somebody gets hurt.
There are frequent breathers, and some longer intervals for dozing in the sunshine. Occasionally they awake to the fact that the
doe of their desire has loped off, and is quarter of a mile ahead.
Then, with no great show of urgency, they catch up and begin
sparring all over again. This may go on for several days. Who is
the actual father of the resultant leverets does not seem to matter. Hares, the enigmas of the countryside, have their own stan-
dards in this respect, and contradictions in others.

Until there is good reason to be otherwise, they are creatures
of habit. Their routes between one feeding area and another are
about as permanent and unalterable as our railway networks.
They are followed generation after generation. Old men on the
farms tell me that they still net hares at the same smeuses
(points where a hare's track leads through a hedge) as easily as
they did in their boyhood half a century ago. Yet in moments of
crisis, or at other times when their thoughts are not preoccupied
by the mating urge, hares can show great presence of mind,
quick improvisation, and subtlety in avoiding danger.

They are not endangered by me. Hares – clean, swift, graceful and mysterious – are one of my fascinations in the hills and fields. Never do I lift a gun against one, though I recognise that some people must do so. Three hares eat as much as one sheep. Until recently the winter hare shoots in the neighbourhood were expected to produce a bag of three hundred per thousand acres. So an uncontrolled hare population would reduce the stock-holding capacity of a medium downland farm by one hundred sheep in the first year, and the number would increase as the enhanced reproduction potential took effect. Latterly, however, the local hare population is less than it was. Fluctuations have always occurred, probably through build-up of liver fluke, and have been self-correcting. But this decline began more suddenly than usual and has lasted longer. I suspect a farm chemical as the cause.

Witchcraft is supposedly a thing of the past. I doubt it. Travelling folk are not alone in having their ideas about the creatures of the day and night even now, as the twentieth century ends. The hare, the large swift-moving hare with the softly glowing eye which appears dramatically from empty ground at dusk and then, almost as suddenly, is no longer there, has been a figure of miracle and mystery since the days of Greek mythology. In these other days of education and television, in which all facts of life are laid bare, a village girl carrying her baby still fears to see a hare. More likely than not, her mother thinks likewise. A hare, the most delicious and nutritious of all our native British game, and enough to provide a succession of family size meals, is no more welcome as a gift than a bunch of peacock feathers in most country homes.

When the game is laid out after a shoot and, in order due, the various participants are invited to take their pick, beaters (recruited from the local folk) generally go to the end of the line where the ground game has been put. They hope for rabbits, a delicacy in the hands of any cottage wife. The rabbits soon go. But when the company has dispersed, when the last headlights light up the trees a mile away, and the last bicycle has jinked down the lane to the village, the hares will still be lying there. I have seen it happen time and again.

"My missus will murder me," keeper after keeper has said, as he loaded them on to his Land-Rover. In most cases, I suspect, his dogs have had them in the end.

The boxing hares turn away lackadaisically over the hill. A more purposeful scene supplants them. Out on a field of winter wheat now springing nicely, two cock pheasants are face to face. They circle watchfully, snaking out their heads each with a wing half-up as guard, seeking a chance to make a stab with beak or spur. They growl at each other, oblivious of me. This is a territorial dispute beyond doubt. The boundary between the estates of two cock pheasants must lie across the field. Man cannot detect, predict or plot exactly where it runs, but the pheasants know to a foot.

On either side of it each must have his nye – the three or four hens which form his harem – and the two cocks are doing what the game cocks do on the halfway line in the farmyard. One pushes his rights beyond the limit, the other resists his claim. Eventually there will be something of a barney, one or the other will withdraw, and peace will be restored. Such is the galliformes' life style, a male-dominated, landed society, with the fallibility imparted by self-interest, and an over-riding recognition that even the most ambitious cannot buck the system.

Territorial rights are its foundation. Once, as I watched from a window, a cock pheasant walked boldly up to a large black tom-cat, peaceably mousing in our paddock, and duffed him up without mercy. The cat jumped on to a fence post, and hissed and spat, but was not followed. I had heard the pheasant growl, and therein found my explanation for its very unpheasantlike choice of opponent. Even cats, among the best informed of animals, do not know everything. This one did not realize that it had elected to stalk mice on the exact but unmarked frontier line of a cock pheasant's territory, its point of minimum toleration.

THE reddened sun sinks in a clear sky as I reach home. The indications are for a clear day tomorrow. And tomorrow the march of Spring takes several backward paces, for I go to fish for salmon.

Not in our home river, where great fish which in their seafaring days have swum to Greenland and back are played ashore to the grass of Wessex meadows, but three hours' drive away on the Welsh March where for a week nearly a mile of the Wye is mine; the Wye which there fulfills a river's destiny by epitomising history; the Wye which comes down from high and lonely places as, in my opinion, a salmon river should.

That most vehement of frontiers, the one between solid Saxon and fiery Celt, is marked on the map half a mile from the inn where I stay. Upstream the Wye is still a Welsh river, charging from the last of its rock-bound gorges into English meadows, its untamed turbulence matching the fervour of the raiders who for centuries sallied down that self-same valley for vengeance and pillage. Here, where place names on the map still tell the story, Saxon pioneering met Cymric pride, and merged in one way or another to make us locals what we are today. From the days of King Offa, who built the great dyke to provide the kind of boundary the pheasants do not need, through the lifetimes of successive Wardens of the Marches to the reign of Edward the First, blood was mingled there on a scale unequalled anywhere in Britain. It proved an explosive flux. Some of it was spilled in conflict; almost every vista on the March includes an ambush point of long ago, or crags once reddened when the fighting stopped. In the intervals of violence, other human forces gave the fusion different form.

When conflict ends, and before it starts again, men and women come together. Generation after generation populated both sides of the March with a distinctive kind of Briton, Saxons impregnated with Celtic fervour and Celts with Saxon tenacity. Their influence spread East and West, leaving still visible imprint on the land. The imprint on history of this blending of the races has been just as positive.

My journey from the southern downland to the Wye takes me

where these things are most obvious. For miles the road leads upwards from Cirencester to the crest of the Cotswold scarp at Birdlip Hill. There the land drops dramatically to a great bowl of countryside as wide as eyes can see. To me it comes near to being a view of heaven while remaining a view of earth. However clear the day, there is nothing in sight which is not the valley of the Severn. This is Sabrina, once the meeting place of two nations, then a birth place of our own, whence has come profound expressions of the English essence, the visions of Shakespeare, the music of Elgar, a great well of Englishness vitalised by Wales.

This is a point which I cannot pass in haste. Short of the Air Balloon, that inn more ancient than its title which has become a landmark for millions, I stop my car and, looking across those glorious miles, feel my sense of Englishness renewed. Had I the ill-luck to die for my country, which on occasions in times past seemed likely to happen, it is for this that I would have done it.

Never twice identical, that scene of grandeur lifts the spirits. In Spring cloud shadows cross the sunlit miles of fields and woods. Far away the landscape details are lost in foreshortened distances beyond which dark hills mark the March. Here we are looking from middle England into Wales – the word that the Saxons in us gave to the land of strangers. In Winter grey clouds come driving over, breaking up in storms, a sight of grim magnificence. Summer revives the coloured counties to the West, patching them with orchards in blossom, and full-leaved trees give roundness and richness to the faraway miles.

I have a vested interest here. The water of the Severn, which shows as broken silver flashes as I look down from Birdlip Hill, is in a sense my blood. Of my thirty-two great-great-great-grandparents, thirty were born and bred in the Severn valley. The interlopers were a Cornishman and a German. In the succeeding generations all my forbears have been long rooted in this great vale where every stream flows eventually to the Severn sea.

It is time to move on. As I drive down the winding hill to Gloucester a sixth sense is at work; the sense of kith. Whatever I am derives from Sabrina, this wide countryside across which I drive. It is homely and peaceful at first, becoming lonely, fierce and haunted towards journey's end.

The Wye, also flowing to the Severn sea, is thus part of it. But the Wye which arrives at Chepstow is very different from the Wye where I shall fish. This river leads a double life, changing its racial identity where it ceases to be a Welsh river and becomes English. I pass Gloucester and signs with peaceful English names; Dean and Ross, St Weonards and Wormelow Tump, Garway and Kentchurch, into the Golden Valley where the hills crowd closer to the road; on beyond Hay, and suddenly the Wye is Welsh. Considering whence it comes, that fact is not remarkable. The demonstration of it is.

The Wye's beginning is on a shoulder of remote Plynlimon, that mountain which more than any other is the shrine of the bardic spirit. They call it Afon Gwy there. Only a mile or two away is the source of the Severn. In two great sweeps the growing rivers part company, break out from the mountains to enclose almost all Sabrina, and join again at the sea. The Severn goes the short way to England, the Wye stays as long as possible in Wales. By one ravine after another, via Llangurig and Rhayader and Builth, it charges through the mountains, as turbulent and beautiful as Welsh poetry and Welsh song and Welsh names, an inspired and untamed river uplifting to the spirits of all who love the truly wild. But where the mountains end the Wye alters too, with dramatic effect.

When in England, do as the English do. Once on the soil of Herefordshire, that august county, dignity replaces hwyl. The Wye suppresses its passion, slows its pace, widens its flow, and the charge becomes a ceremonial march. Through the stately landscape the Wye takes a correspondingly stately course, bland now instead of tempestuous, assured instead of rebellious. The place names on its banks no longer bespeak Celtic rhythms; instead the leisured heritage from centuries of English prosperity – Hereford, Monmouth, Symond's Yat and Tintern, then the sea.

The salmon which I hope to catch nearly all first swam in the Welsh reaches, in small streams above the 1,000 ft contour, bubbling through the ling and rushes on misty hills loud with sheep and curlews. Their ancestors had likewise all begun life there too. Every salmon which goes down to the sea returns to breed in the river where it was itself hatched, not making the mistake of swimming up the Severn instead of the Wye for instance, even though they share a common estuary, and even though the eventual destination might be only twenty minutes apart for a ranging sheepdog. In the meantime every seafaring British salmon has made a sea trip of at least seven thousand miles. Whether crossing the Atlantic, helped by oceanic gyres, or the mountaineering feat of re-ascending the parent river, is the greater achievement may be debatable. But I have often thought that a salmon which survives all the attendant perils and then makes the eventual misjudgment of taking my fly and being hooked, killed, and eaten as a result, is entitled to a little sympathy. Well, perhaps.

There are two ways of looking at it. Except for us fishermen, and the money we pay for the right to fish, there would be neither incentive nor money to keep rivers clean, peaceful and unobstructed so that the salmon born in them could return to them and breed. Nor would there be protection for the young salmon which as fry and parr and smolts spend three years in their parent rivers growing large enough for sea life, facing the hazards of attack by seals, and the trawl-nets and long-lines of fishermen from twenty other nations.

Our salmon, Atlantic salmon, are very special fish, unique and not to be confused with the Pacific salmon which finish in tins on supermarket shelves. There are plenty of those, but not plenty of ours. Paradoxically the only way to ensure their survival is to continue catching them; not too many, but enough to give them a value so that they continue to be too considerable an asset for the consumer society to render extinct. If nobody values them, nobody will protect them. Fortunately, the day when our salmon values become more realistic is not now far away.

It is now possible to farm salmon in the sea, enclosing them in safety, cutting out the transatlantic migration and the risk of interception by seals and of being scooped out by trawlers asset-stripping on the migration routes. Farmed salmon in bulk quantities would take the rarity value out of the species and by bringing their price down, remove the profit from salmon exploitation. In addition (self-interest rears its ugly head) salmon angling would be an uncomplicated sport again, not inflated by commercial pressures. This would pose no threat to the species; nor did it, before fortuitous mappings of the migration journeys enabled non-producing nations to put a stranglehold on our salmon's sea routes. Rod-fishing is an enjoyable but highly inefficient means of catching salmon. In the most successful seasons the total catch by rods does not approach one-tenth of the total recorded commercial catch by the nets nationwide, to which must be added the international maritime sea catches, of which little is known for certain except that they are enormous.

These things being so, it is sometimes suggested that it would be a good thing if (perhaps only as a gesture) some of us ceased to fish for salmon for a time – me, for instance. And, if this would be a good idea, why do I not act accordingly and give my salmon rod a rest? Perhaps it would not be greatly to the advantage of the salmon if I did. This is another question to which there are many sides.

I have a Hindu friend who says that Destiny puts a quota on all our pleasures. So we start life with, as it were, a ration of satisfactions ahead of us, varied according to our tastes and environment, and according to the way the gods have biassed our desires – so many tigers, so many buffalo, so many women, so many magnums of port, so much money, so many salmon, stags, pheasants, grouse – the list is endless. As we fulfill each quota the desire for more fades, so men turn to their other options, taking up as yet unexhausted pleasures with zest renewed. To me the idea is an attractive exposition of his ancient philosophy, which is in essence joy in life; and my experience suggests it has some truth.

My salmon quota was evidently rather low. I do not know how many I have caught, but the total must be small compared to that of many men known to me. I have had my four before lunch, my six in a day, and a trickle over the seasons. Now, when the trickle ceases, I no longer feel frustration, or any sense of unrequited desire. It cannot greatly matter if I never catch another salmon. My quota is probably exhausted. My friends, who have caught many more salmon than I, and still go avidly out for more, must have begun with larger quotas than I. This being so, a personal state of no more salmon would not bring deprivation.

But the quota applies to salmon catching, not to salmon fishing, for the pleasures of which the salmon itself is only the polarisation. They are sensuous, based on contact with the elements of wind, water, weather and terrain. Salmon fishing, its climaxes apart, is something which one feels as much as does; it can never be said to be all in the mind. Here, this evening in late March, my travels ended for the day, the challenge of tomorrow is taking shape and the instincts of a Winter man are ready to respond. Spring takes a pace backward here.

Because the general drift of our weather is West to East, ours being an island in an atmospheric overflow of the Atlantic into Europe, the Welsh March lies in the meteorological shadow of Wales. The mountains funnel harsh winds downwards into the English plain, dropping their overplus of snow. The rivers rise and roar in time of storm. Those who think of fishing in terms of peace and rest, of the contemplative man's recreation, and other conventional misnomers would have no place here. To say that they would be out of their depth has a grim significance. This kind of fishing is for those who are fit enough, able to take care of themselves.

Below the bridge the river tells me it is running high, a shade too high, but running down. The line of its retreat is still damp along the far bank. The fall may well be only temporary, but at least offers hope for next day. I go on to the inn, off-load, sign the book, and dissolve the memory of the miles in a pint of bitter beer. Others of the party are also checking in. The cellar will soon be under pressure.

"Wonder what port they've got," says somebody with his mind on the back-up to the stuff of life. I leave him turning the leaves of the wine list, rapt as a monk at his breviary.

A Raven at the River

Morning brings a hard, chill blow. The river is down a little further and now holding steady, says the watcher. Fish are up, more than one hundred and fifty river miles already behind them, so we have a chance. But this is not a fishing story, just the story of an occasional fisherman, and of what is in it for him.

Desolation, for instance. This is hard country; the pasture more fit for geese than beasts, so close-bitten that it looks shaved as I walk to my beat. In the strip of woodland above the fishing hut the ground is naked, not carpeted as it is near home. Winter wind-blows felled three large trees, tearing the roots from their stoney holds and leaving them reared high above my head. There is a rushing sound from the river, now in sight one hundred feet below, curling and creaming round its boulders, then fanning out and slowing down into a long pool below, then gathering speed again, flowing onwards furiously towards England and the sea.

The hut has had a narrow escape. The line of debris marking the highest of the spate is only a foot or so lower than its step. From below comes an evil smell. A drowned sheep lies on the shingle there, mouth gaping, staring blindly. The crows have had its eyes and tongue. I find a spot upwind to tackle-up and don my waders, taking my time, testing each knot, letting the tumbled rocks, the bleak air and the hungry river draw me into their company, making me a part of their bare scene.

Beyond the far bank, the hard features of Winter have not yet relaxed. South-west, the Brecon Beacons are barred with snow. The wind comes from there – thin and freezing, worth a guinea a minute. Overhead a buzzard mews. Before lunch I shall have heard the bass voice of a raven, driven by hope of better pickings to leave the high crags deep in Wales and lend his magisterial presence to dignify the flocks of lesser scavengers wherever flowing water concentrates the misfortunes of others. Crows, magpies and jackdaws patrol the riverside, knowing that the falling level will leave corpses stranded – anything between drowned rats, birds or rabbits and occasional bullocks islanded by spates and carried, helpless, downstream.

With rod assembled and all equipment checked, it is time to wade in at the head of the long pool. The nearer to the water, the less one can hear of things outside it. The river's voice shouts down all else. Its roar and churning, trapped and echoed back by the sides of the ravine, imprison me. Now I am not only in the presence but in the power of an ever moving, implacable, irresistible force millions of years old; the river.

Though a much used road runs within two hundred yards, no traffic can be heard. A bulling heifer which had been holding forth as I came to the hut is out of earshot now, as suddenly as if switched off, so is the birdsong from the strip of woodland. I shall go all day without hearing aircraft, something which is impossible anywhere else than beside a river. Yet water noise has the selective quality of letting through some sounds smaller than those which it obliterates. Until I hear its rasping chirp I do not see a dipper bobbing black and white on a mid-stream rock only fifteen yards from my right elbow. And all the morning, deafened to much else, I still hear the faraway barking of a sheepdog whose master has gone to the hill without him.

Other senses than hearing must also come to terms with wading a big river. The related sense of balance is one of them. Every stride into that flood reminds me of it. Our balance mechanism is in our ears, but our eyes can negate it. Thigh-deep in moving water now, and soon to be deeper still, no solid ground in sight, the time comes when I must be careful in lifting my eyes. They, calibrated on the water surface as it races away, its wavelets and its spray ceaselessly hurrying forward, register stationary objects as tilting backwards. The ravine here is deep, tree-clad on one bank. The narrow strip of sky, the pine tops, the rock faces, even myself, all seem to be heeling over. The temptation is to correct this by leaning forward, almost an invitation to dive in. I must make a conscious effort not to. In time my reflexes will adapt; provided, of course, that I keep my feet.

Every fisherman has learned that one of life's half-truths is to know a river by sight. One knows the whole of it only by going into it. The Wye is then revealed as a sly customer, emphatically not to be trusted. Most of its bed in these its upper reaches consists of rolling stones, football diameter or smaller (skull-sized, as a ghillie once dispiritingly described them to me)

smoothed and rounded by endless water friction. Stones are relatively lighter when submerged, and only a touch is needed to
set these moving. Sometimes all the stones on which one stands
move in unison, so that the river bed behaves like an escalator.
Since gravity takes them towards the depths at its centre, a
fishermen is then carried across the flow. Then the senses of
balance, sight and feeling, the latter via the feet, convey conflict-
ing signals to the brain; dizziness follows, and the danger that
looms becomes actual, not merely potential.

Wise men do not wade the Wye with fewer than three legs,
the third being a wading staff. Mine is hornbeam, iron-shod and
lead-weighted to keep its foot well down in fast water. It is
attached to me by a leather harness, so that I can let go of it
when I need both hands to fish. At other times I can use it as an
ice-axe is used when snow slips on a mountain, to anchor me
until the bottom has ceased moving, or to steady me as I move
one of my legs forward or back to adjust balance, to change
position, or to open up an angle for the next cast. The rule of
life is never to trust it to a single contact with the rocks. If I lift
either foot, the staff reinforces the other.

Having eased out to the neck of the pool, I pause a while.
Only when the surroundings have ceased their tipsy canting and
leaning is it safe to fish. To start too soon and hook a salmon at
first cast, would be a happening so rare that to drown through
loss of balance, hence unable to tell the tale, would be a great
pity.

All else apart, I should miss a day of this mysterious solitary
joy, alone and deeper now in the rushing water where the weight
of the Wye clasps me at the waist, shoving and bunting and
sucking at me, as if in a sincere desire to wrench me loose, bowl
me over and sweep me down to the Severn sea. Like that sea,
the river is an enemy and the first contest is between me and it,
not between me and the salmon. I go down into it, and I come
back; that is the shape of salmon-fishing days. It is not quite a
certainty.

On a lower beat, I fished in years past with the river watcher
as ghillie. Whenever we passed a little pool where an alder tree

65

leaned over, he would lift his cap with the incantation, "A fine fisher, and a good man". A local doctor had drowned there in his boyhood forty years before. This kind of fishing is a risk sport. I believe in the therapeutic value of risk within reason, a little bit but not too much. Risk, and the awareness of it, has shaped all life, ourselves included. Its total absence means the prison, the asylum, the inner city, or any other syndrome of deprivations in which life degenerates to mere existence. Risk keeps us alert, makes us responsible, stops us being big-headed, reminds us that even in a twentieth century Welfare State the forces of Nature are greater than we are.

The other contest, between me and the salmon, is still to come, even though I am now in the water and already fishing. The executive decision that it shall start lies with the salmon, not with me. Until one of them decides to take my fly there can be no contact between us. Salmon fishing, as distinct from salmon catching consists of the presentation of the fly to the fish in the manner that makes it most likely to be taken.

In theory, the morality of salmon fishing stands a little higher than that of trout fishing, which is undeniably an exercise in false pretences. Trout are caught when, in the course of feeding, they are offered a counterfeit fly, containing a hook, resembling the species of insect for which at that moment they are seen to be hungry. Salmon, however, are not feeding at the time of capture. Having returned from the sea, they never feed in fresh water. A salmon does not take a fly because it needs to eat but because in an unguarded moment, anger, curiosity, cupidity or destructiveness has undermined its judgment. Salmon which are caught invite their fate by their own folly and the salmon-fisher's strategy is to exploit their rashness, as I am doing now. My fly must capture the attention of any salmon lying in the pool below, and incite one of them to yield to impulse. Seductively, irritatingly, even threateningly, it must enter not only their environment but their consciousness, and be made to behave in a way that they cannot ignore until one of them, impelled by jealousy or who knows what other motivation, forgets himself and attacks.

If he does, I have as good as got him – provided I keep my head and my feet, anticipate all contingencies, and handle my tackle properly. Landing a salmon is a much more manageable operation than hooking one, but a fisherman who spends as much as one per cent of his salmon time in playing fish is doing twice as well as I hope to do, on average, throughout my life. If the only pleasure were in the catching, the time factor would be prohibitive for most of us.

To me, the incidental pleasures are greater than the moments of triumph. The thrills of being where I am are doubled by the physical pleasure of what I am about to. My salmon rod creates stresses and rhythms which make it as inspiring as a partner in a dance. The forces which I put into it through my arms, shoulders, back and legs are given back to me by the rod, so that I must respond again; and again and again *ad infinitum* with timing, judgment and touch. A salmon rod is neither a labour-saving implement nor an inert tool. This continued repetition during long days on a river creates the contentment which comes from efficient performance as well as the well-being which always follows effort. Salmon or no salmon, those rewards are certain.

My salmon rod is ten feet and six inches long, therefore shorter than most. In that length there are latent strengths – some natural, some built-in – as if it has life of its own. Indeed it once had. Its life began as natural cane, growing beside the South China sea. Imported here it was split lengthways and its segments shaped, then re-assembled in a form both tapered and balanced. If, thirty years after, it still has residual life (I believe it does) the rod-maker has redistributed it in three sections so that it serves my purposes. The butt, the section which when in action lies between my wrists, is strong but not rigid, a firm base for the exertion of power. The centre section contains the strength, flexing and recuperating in action, building up and multiplying its acquired energy, taking what I give it and demanding more. From the top section, lissom and delicate, comes accuracy in the fall of line, and sensitivity to my touch.

How easy it looks to a watcher on the bank, viewing side-on.

The seemingly leisured sweeping of the rod in which timing conceals exertion, the symmetrical flow, forward-and-back and forward-and-back, of forty yards of line, cutting into the wind, dropping so that the pool is systematically quartered. Sometimes a flick cast sends it rolling down the river in hoops, spinning off sparkling droplets, then straightening out to send the fly darting forward like an adder's tongue. There is a mastery about it now which I enjoy the more by remembering the days when I could not. No mastery then; instead a rod which answered back, bullying and kicking against my unpractised efforts to use it; a line which behaved like a rebellious snake; hands that blistered, and a back that ached. All that is over now. Here, in this resounding gorge amid the leaping water, my rod and I are in unison, and five-eighths of my thought is with my fly as I move two strides down the pool after each cast.

On this grey day I have put up a Thunder-and-Lightning, responsive to the stormy sky. It is tied with moose hair by a Canadian friend, a more subtle searcher-out under fast water than the feathered versions more usual here. When the line drops I feel the river take possession of it, linking me to that racing, foam-flecked flood which is the spirit of Wales heading for the bland shires of England as the spirit of Wales has always done, though nowadays its impact has been reduced to Rugby football. Somewhere, under the swirling surface, the Thunder-and-Lightning is at work, swinging as slowly as I can make it across the noses of any salmon waiting there below – enticing, tantalising and, with luck, attracting. Up the line, through the slim rod-tip, down to my hand, I can feel the pull of the water and the small vibrations which mark the fly's passage. Sometimes I must mend the cast a little to take the fly down deeper to where the fish may be, near the bottom, each sheltered by a boulder from the press of water coming down. They wait their chance to run on upstream to small streams on the misty heights where their lives began, and most of them will end.

The Wye gives little warning of that moment. Somewhere higher up, nearer Aberystwyth than any other recognisable place, Atlantic vapour blows hard against Welsh hills, and spills its cargo of rain. The streams gather it, feeding it into tributaries and so to the river which forthwith dispatches it down. Then things happen so quickly that fishermen may have only minutes to reach safety.

Something indescribable about the water gives me the first clue. It gurgles in a different tone perhaps. Whatever the signal, it forewarns me. When the pressure point of the water on my waders is suddenly a perceptible inch higher above my waist the realization comes not as news but as confirmation. The river is coming up, and I am getting out, reeling in and using my three-legged watermanship to cross the rolling stones to the bank.

It is colder here. The water was warmer than the air, as it often is in March. The fishing hut calls, with its soup, sausages, cheese and beer. A company of enterprising birds assembles; finches, tits and tree-sparrows. They recognise a free meal when they see one. To the first cock chaffinch (has the world a bird more beautiful than this confection of pastel blue, pink and buff, black and white?) I flick a crumb of cheese. This is the quickest taming act in all wild life. He picks it up, and another. Thereafter he cannot take his eyes off me. On our fifth day he sits on my hat as I fish, speaking the logo which gives him his name of spink here on the March.

From the warmth of the inn, we hear the river roaring through the night. For the first hour of its rising all life around it had woken up as the salmon abandoned their lies and prepared to move on. In the excitement of the new urge to travel, two threw caution aside and paid the penalty and, when the level ran down again, two more, one to me. Now my back is to the river and the car is turned homeward-bound across Sabrina, back to Wessex, and other rites of Spring.

Few journeys nowadays are pleasures in themselves; most are merely changes of location to be endured and then forgotten. But this journey weaves its magic either way. The March, its mountains and the golden gorse fall behind. The road crosses the red soil of Herefordshire, flanked by rich farms and hopyards. Pokes, great sacks which will hold the hop harvest, are being washed and pegged out to dry. On their billowing shapes I read names that have slaked a million throats – Marcle, Trumpet, Grandison, Ocle Pychard, Marden and Westhide, all honoured progenitors in the pedigree of beer. To the right are more signposts to the Wye's English reaches; no rebel torrent now but a dignified waterway linking Hampton Bishop, Holme Lacey, Fownhope, the Dean and Chapter pool and Kerne, where Robert Pashley, the great angler, lived. He was credited with ten thousand salmon and was still eager for more, which shows how unequally the gods allot their quotas of desire. I do not envy him. There are other things in life for which a man who caught so many salmon could not have time.

All around me in my mile-a-minute progress are the creamy names of other villages in England's most contented county. Northward, just discernible for a few miles, rise the tawny hills of Shropshire, whence I came. But that is a story for later. Ahead lies the climb back up to Birdlip. There, when the last glimpse of Sabrina is lost astern, the spell is ended. Back, in my non-ancestral, adopted country of Wessex, the future takes shape.

NO gathering in a British year is more of a pleasure to join than the crowd at a point-to-point. Nowhere are people in better humour, more considerate, better looking, or more mixed and yet the same – each individual point-to-point crowd, while including the whole gamut of contrasting humanity, being exactly like all the others. Nowhere does one see so many healthy complexions, those of the ladies owing little to art but occasionally something to the bottle in the case of their escorts. Wind and sunshine, storm and tempest, are great aids to beauty and in the informality and self-confidence of these friendly multitudes human values stand revealed. Everybody is assured of his or her knowledge, interest, and place in the scheme of things. These are no strangers here, nobody is out of his element.

The assembled grannies, looking like Women's Institute grass roots, know the horse form to the ounce. There are old and rustic gentlemen, between whom flasks pass as deftly as the ball among French rugby players, who converse in tones expanded by lifetimes of chat across wide acres. Schoolgirls argue odds with bookmakers, are seen off and try again. Magnates with costly binoculars hail, on brotherly terms, homespun men wearing shirts without collars. Mothers curse children without inhibition. Fathers go missing. About fifty per cent of the gathering are visitors from towns who "would not miss it for anything". All human life is here.

The course is an abstract concept, except for the jumps and the finishing straight. Even in the late twentieth century there are still nineteenth century harvest wagons on which to put the judge, the stewards, and such members of the general public as have the brass neck to get up beside them. Bells jangle, a hunting horn is blown, marker flags stretch in the wind. As things have been, most of them remain.

The smell of bruised grass, released by the coming and going of countless feet on turf, is among them. As always, smell is the most evocative of the senses and, as they say, it takes me back. My brief, undistinguished part in point-to-points ended years ago. Seeing the expertise of modern point-to-points it is hard to believe that I was ever part of them. Until I smell bruised grass.

Then, as if the blood of youth had been renewed, all is real again. I know what the gladiators of today are thinking. Amid the crowds and the uproar, those saddles are lonely places. They are also unfriendly, hard and cold to thin-clad thighs, and in odd contrast to the warm and vibrant thoroughbreds under them. Among those self-assured young men and women is doubtless one (human nature does not change) who, feeling the uncertainties and self-doubts that I did, notes that the horse is not similarly troubled. Cocked ears, a strong hold on the bit, a great machinery of lungs and muscles that power the tattoo of hooves below, combine to restore a rider's waning faith. The first jump, suddenly near, vanishes beneath the surging leap. Then six or seven mad minutes of total release. The crash and curses at the fences, the thudding drum-beat gallop, rushing wind, whistling divots flung back from those in front, heaving breath, and then with luck the blurred crowd, the cheering, and the pull-up past the post.

Without luck, it is oblivion and that old bouquet, bruised grass, again. And the fatherly arms of St John's Ambulance men, with their injunction to "Take it easy, son" – son being in no state to take it any other way when the role was played by me. So, when somebody else hits the deck, I know what it smells like (though not what it feels like, because it is never twice the same). Better than any sal volatile is that aromatic blend of chlorophyll and damp earth, the first intimation of the surrounding world to him who regains consciousness. The occasional extra redolence of a butcher's shop is no more than one's own contribution by way of a bleeding nose. That is one way of remembering the days of my youth, and I do not suppose I am alone in it.

All that remains of it now is the basic fragrance, with its reminder that the rest is in the past for me. I admit feeling comfort, not regret, that there is no more wondering how I talked myself into being in this situation, in a paddock, wearing garish clothes, waiting on a freezing day to ride a far from reassuring looking horse against the even less reassuring rivals that dot the enclosure around me – a rough lot if ever I saw one. To be frank, the real answers to that question were diverse, and doubtless remain so still. Bravado, a need for self-proof, a desire to impress the girls (few better ways exist), fear of saying No when asked, a faith in one's prospects which soon evaporated but was genuine for a time.

Standing now beside the rail, I look at those who are about to do battle, and mentally lift my cap. Point-to-points are not for the half-hearted. A senior kinsman, who had a distinguished record under Rules, warned me off them. "Very risky," he said. Asked if steeplechases were not very risky too, he talked down their element of relative hazard. He considered point-to-points too dangerous for a man of prudence, and flatly refused to compete. It was wiser to ride races against professionals. They rode against each other every day and had their living to earn. If they got ironed-out no money came in. When a point-to-pointer is decanted, somebody else milks the cows, drives the tractor, runs the practice, keep the books, or whatever. So professionals, while averse to making life easy for opponents, observed certain safety practices. Point-to-pointers, he considered, either do not or cannot or both; and in any case, for those out for glory not hard cash, there is no incentive to.

That was in times past. I do not believe attitudes have altered, though the game itself has. Competition is immensely more keen now, expertise much greater, the opposition more sophisticated, more purposive, less local. The horses have still, supposedly, been "regularly and fairly hunted during the current season" but the chance of meeting in point-to-points steeplechase stars of recent memory is everyday experience now, not the rarity it was, though of course it always happened. To prove that there is nothing new under the sun, the Crimean War had only just ended when Adam Lindsay Gordon sent-up the hunter certificate of his day in the lines,

> He calls "hunted fairly" a horse that has barely
> Been stripped for a trot within sight of the hounds,
> A horse that at Warwick beat Birdlime and Yorick,
> And gave Abd-el-Kadir at Aintree nine pounds.

The Masters of Foxhounds who sign hunters' certificates for such horses nowadays are doing nothing new, only more often.

The present scene is fired by the old simplicities: first past the stick, and the devil take the rest. But there are two specific changes. The ladies have come in, and some of the tradition has gone out. Of course, there have always been ladies' races in my lifetime, but they used to be light relief rather than serious business. The lady riders of today are so capable and so brave that ladies' races now rank higher than most. And since the riders may be weighing out at 10 stone 7 lbs instead of 12 stone, they

are run faster than most. And when those self-same ladies compete on equal terms with men they pep up the standard of competition instead of watering it down.

There were minor pomps about the old ways which I miss.
Though my generation rode in colours, many meetings included
a Hunt race "to be ridden in hunting costume" as the official
wording had it. Those of insufficient gravitas did not dare to
enter, so the event was left to those who could comport themselves with dignity in red coat, top hat and a racing saddle. Most
of them were hard men to hounds four days a week all winter,
their red coats not what they purported to be but light-weight
versions leaving plenty of freedom for arms and shoulders, and
liberties could not be taken in their company. The qualification
for those who rode in other races was they should be "gentlemen
qualified to do so, or their sons". Many and varied were the
stratagems employed to penetrate this agreeably elastic wording.
All I can say is that I succeeded, perhaps because I posed little
threat to anybody. In any sport, losers are always welcome.

One comfort (in the word's old sense) in a point-to-point is
togetherness. As a race develops, so does the rigour of the game.
But when the flag falls, all set off together, all for the moment
equal, the galloping mass giving to its component individals the
optimism of safety in numbers. Riders in a hunter trial need a
colder courage, for they go singly, passing alone the fraught
seconds of the count-down in the roped-off starting box, then
tackling the course singly. Here I am more closely involved.

Backing-up a daughter, I have done my stuff loading and
unloading the horse-box, tacking-up, leading up the horse before
and after warm-up, getting horse and rider to the collecting ring
on time. Now there is nothing left to do but that most arid of
human duties, to watch. A hunter trial is not a race, except with
the stop-watch. The young, the brave, and the ultra-competitive
are here in force. There are bonus points for the speed section
and all will go for any they can get. Our tactics have been
planned, and now ... four, three, two, one ... the solemn voice
tolls the last mental seconds but zero is never reached. The flag
falls, the black horse is away as if this is the Ascot five furlongs.

For a time we can follow her; up a long slope, along a shoulder of bare hill, then round a wood into dead ground. Down come the binoculars. No point in looking for a bit. "Cup of coffee?" The question, superbly timed by the flask-holder, slackens the tension. "Yes, thanks; just time." While I drink it, I do my own count-down in my head. I pass the cup back and there she is, right on cue, a black dot three-quarters of a mile away, heading back to us, going strong. Six more jumps and she comes through the finish. It's a moment every parent knows.

She dismounts. I take the horse. "Good show," her mother says.

"Not fast enough," she answers, "but it was great. Julia was in front of me, and she was quicker. I think Robin caught up a bit too."

"Never mind," we say, "you can still be third."

'What's third?"

BACK home, the clouds are high and wide apart, sailing over from the South like a fleet. Between them the sun lights up the fields, woods, houses and gardens. The earth, and all that is on it, soak up the elixir of fertility and growth. There are blue-bells flowering in our wild garden, tulips and narcissi in the borders. A swallow sings on the stable power-line, others reconnoitre the hay bay for nest sites, a great tit repeats his theme song, a chiff-chaff calls above the bluebells, a marsh warbler pours his heart out, and over the fields where growing hay sweetens the breeze a cuckoo calls.

This is the English Spring, caught in a rare moment when it is neither disappointing us nor making false promises. The year has thrown away its sting. When Spring touches such perfection we are moving into Summer, and towards fishing in a lusher setting. The quarry now is trout, the scene the rich and gentle South. It is a different sport, with different motivations from the rugged challenge which salmon presented in the clamorous defiles of Wales.

The path to the water leads from the road across three single-plank bridges, the sort which are part of the Wessex scene. Where valleys widen, rivers were long ago split into carriers, taking their water to irrigate pastures ever further from the parent stream, and needing to be crossed at intervals. Every bridge plank is covered with wire-netting, nailed tightly to it lest feet should slip on timber treacherous after rain. The length of wire-netting on Wessex bridges must total many miles, and time expended on fixing it, and re-fixing it after winter damage, thousands of man-hours. Yet I do not know of a Wessex foot-bridge unwired. And who does this noble work for the betterment of mankind while fishing? The landlords, of course. That much-abused elite make life easier and safer for the rest of us in this and other ways. At each bridge I stop to weigh up the form. What goes on in a carrier is a fair guide to prospects in the main river.

At the first bridge little goes on. I am not depressed. Being the outermost tentacle, the flow here is slowest, the weed build-up greatest and, only yards from the B road where my car is parked, the most disturbed by passers-by, not all of whom are innocent sightseers. When the water bailiff is safely identified somewhere else, opportunistic poachers get busy, well aware of the ease of access and get-away.

At the second bridge I think I see the flick of a departing tail. But it is not worth waiting to confirm the observation. There is no public right of way here and the stalwart form of a Friesian bull shows up in the field beyond among a bunch of heifers a hundred yards to the left of the line from bridge to bridge. He ought to have enough on his mind to leave him disinterested in me, but would-be survivors do not take risks with bulls of dairy breeds. By their descent from top-class milk-producing cows they inherit the highly-strung, intolerant tempers of creative workers. So I give dairy bulls as wide a berth as possible, and cross the next meadow before this one comes nearer.

With one more carrier to cross, I can take my time. I spend it watching a three-pound fish high in the water twenty-five yards upstream. He is golden flanked and spotted like a leopard. Occasionally he eases upwards and sips something downwards off the water surface, which he scarcely disturbs. Every minute or so a puff of wind blows catspaws over him, and I lose sight of him. But when the view clears the golden patch is still there and forms itself into a fish – a wholesome, athletic, and most desirable fish indeed.

The cupidity aroused in men by the sight of a fish in water seems basic to our psyches. The intensity of my own reaction surprises me. The determination to possess it is overwhelming and irrational, far transcending, too, any value that the fish may have, and irrespective of my own lack of need of it. Perhaps fish were the staple food of our remote ancestors, and we are heirs to their response to the sight of any fish which might be brought within our reach. I have reflected long upon this strange, widely shared obsession.

When I see a pheasant within gunshot I take care not to miss. But if in fact I do miss, my sense of failure is transient. I wish the pheasant good luck, and watch for another. I am not left shocked, angry at my inadequacy, shaken and sweating in anticlimax. Yet this is the effect on me of failing to hook or land a trout which I have stalked successfully (perhaps for an hour or more) and, by accurate casting, tempted into rising to my fly. So near and yet so far. Even if only for a split second, there will have been contact between us. I could and should have brought it into possession. Instead the severance, the death of hope, the bleak proof of failure, the unarguable truths that I was inadequate, that my own ineptitude and nothing else deprived me of the fish I determined to catch, and that a better man would have caught it (and probably will). All combine to magnify the feelings of frustration and despair. Why should it be so important?

No such powerful feelings are produced by the larger and more portentous salmon. But the fisherman does not see the salmon until after he has hooked it. The dry-fly fisherman does see the trout, in isolation and at length, marking it out from among other possibles as his target fish. What the eye has not seen, the heart does not grieve over; the saying has some application here. Each of us must react in our individual ways to our high moments and our low moments; to me, no low moment in any other sport or game is so lowering as failure to catch a trout which, in angling parlance, I have "touched".

A missed putt at golf is the result of miscalculation; as old Omar said of polo, "the ball no answer makes of ayes and noes, but right or left, as strikes the player, goes". To this wisdom of the East fly-fishers likewise have no answer, but have wind, and water drag, and obstacles as mitigating factors. A dropped catch at cricket, an open goal missed at soccer or a fumbled pass at rugby are all very annoying, as the rest of the team make plain. But none contain those bitter elements of introspective loss of face caused by the contemptuous departure of a good trout which has defeated me. All handicaps have been overcome and every detail of judgment and dexterity successfully achieved, except the last one.

In that situation I wade to the bank and climb out, drained of hope, energy, self-respect, and initiative, as inert as if concussed. In times past I would mobilise my last dregs of strength of purpose, and light a pipe. The hand that held the match would tremble. Now I merely sit down and contemplate the vacuum that life has then become. After a while, like an automaton, I move on to seek another fish, telling myself meanwhile that there is no point in the business anyway, and I might as well give it up. Hours later, after some unsensed moment of transition of which I have never yet been conscious, I again find my whole soul committed to the capture of an equally desirable fish, my body poised, my muscles tempered, my eyes prepared, my wrist cocked. We fishermen plunge from triumph to disaster, but we also soar from disaster back to triumph.

No wonder that those who do not follow our strange pastime

Mary Scott

cannot understand its spell. Some aspects of it are always more important to me than catching fish. They include the long solitudes, release from cares which in other environments loom large, absorption into Nature, and that separation from time which makes Nature eternal. Here near the Old Barge, on the Itchen below Winchester, the union is complete.

This is where medieval monks, long before the carriers were dug, divided the stream to prevent traffic jams among the cargo boats which then navigated it. To ease the upstream passage of laden craft from Southampton they made a by-pass, straight as a Roman road, where the river's course curved inconveniently. Seven centuries have passed since they did it, but still the banks they made are firm; and still part of the river follows its former bed, tortuously but close alongside. No goods have been hauled up-river for many generations past. Trout have it almost to themselves. And one of the last boats, which ran aground on this stretch and rotted away with the years, gave it the name it bears.

On the carrier bridge, watching the trout of the moment, wind is on my face – where a fly-fisher least wants it. To propel an artificial fly, made of feather and silk on a tiny steel hook, through a wall of oncoming air is not only difficult but a contradiction of Nature; and if it is to fall into the trout's field of surface vision the margin for error at twenty-five yards is about four inches. I decide against it. A clumsy cast would scare the fish away to no purpose. But if I leave him undisturbed, and if the wind drops, I can return. Fly-fishing is full of ifs.

On the main river no spreading circles yet show where trout have taken flies. So then begins that pleasurable fishing interlude, waiting for something to happen. Soon it becomes a listening to what is happening. The wrenching cry of a dabchick comes from a willow clump, the cooing of wood-pigeons from some tall alders nodding against the sky. I hear a blackbird, a reed-warbler, and the whisper of a willow-tit. A kingfisher speeds upstream like a jewelled flash.

Where every prospect pleases, some people would say that only man is vile. Not I. The presence, in such a scene as this, of

man and his work need not be discordant. The setting belongs
to us, and we belong in it. Long ago I achieved notoriety by
mentioning in print that I had hung a transistor radio from a
tree and, while I fished, listened to Schumann's Third Symphony. I would do so again rather than miss either that glorious
music, or half an hour on an equally glorious river. I wondered
at the time how many of my outraged critics would have recognised it, or understood that it was composed in praise of another
river, the Rhine. I wonder still at the strange mentality of those
who believe that humanity's varied forms of uplift must necessarily be enjoyed one at a time, instead of together, enhancing
each other.

On this day two rivers are to combine to enhance my pleasure
in fishing. When the fly begins to hatch, and tell-tale circles
reveal which fish are taking, the Itchen yields me four trout, the
smallest a pound and a half. I kill them without remorse, for I
am predator and do not mind admitting it. Nearly everybody
nowadays is a predator, but some of this great majority are
holier-than-thou in not admitting it. They prefer to claim the
non-existent virtue of not taking life while indulging themselves,
sometimes grossly, in the results of killing done by others on
their behalf. The harmony of this day is not disturbed for me by
my doing what the pike and the heron do. Having thought the
question through, I face its realities.

If the only pleasure for me in fishing were the feel of a hooked
fish fighting for its life I would give it up. To catch fish and then
return them to the water, to provide this sensation for other
fishermen again and again (as is done with coarse fish, perhaps
must be done so that all who wish may have a share in the sport)
does not attract me. Neither does the claim to be exercising
mercy convince me. I kill, and when I kill, I or somebody else
eats what I kill in the natural order of predation as advocated
by the angel to St Peter in the Acts of the Apostles.

The trout that I have seen, stalked, caught by the skill of my
hand and the exercise of my wits, will in due course emerge from
my deep-freeze to nourish me, my family, and our guests. When
I turn away from the secretive Itchen, hidden among its trees

81

and reed beds, the struggles of those four fish and my trivial triumphs in catching them, are only incidental memories. What I have gained is neither them nor the sweet smell of success, but the invigoration of going back to Nature by spending half a day in that separate world, fulfilling the human role in Creation.

Afternoon is deepening towards evening when the time comes for me to leave for the Test, the other of Hampshire's geological miracles. Chalk streams are giant springs, not dependent on tributaries or direct replenishment by rain for their flow, but formed of water which fell months previously, percolated downwards through the chalk, gathered in subterranean reservoirs and waterways which we call aquifers, and reappeared as rivers through other faults in the chalk overlay. Like the carriers on the surface, the aquifers control the flow underground. So chalk streams do not flood, and seldom run thin or become coloured. Descent through the chalk filters their water and impregnates it with minerals which cause their weed to grow lushly, and the fly larvae, crustaceans and molluscs which live in it to thrive. Hence the vigour of chalk stream life-chains ending, at the top of the pyramid, with those paladins of their species, chalk-stream trout.

The sun is well past the yard-arm, gilding the Itchen water, when I decide to make the change. There is no activity now, no rise-forms made by feeding trout, and most birdsong has ceased. A moorhen crosses the glide upstream. Amid the surrounding silence, three coots are in noisy dispute, like boys playing in an empty church. The river, and all the life in and beside it, has begun its daily siesta – the quiet hour before a new awakening. I fill it with the journey, river to river, along lanes over which shadows lengthen.

Identical as they are in form the world's two most famous trout streams, Test and Itchen, have contrasting personalities. Itchen is feminine, as beguiling as a subtle, witty woman and as cautious in dispensing favours. Test is masculine but placid, enigmatic as a mandarin passing by inscrutably. The quiet fields are sweet with baled hay as I make what must be a fly-fisherman's most idyllic journey from one river to the other, thinking of what is past, planning for what I am about to do.

The Test is always a challenge, which tonight I shall meet in specialised form. My invitation is to the most renowned of all carriers, Ginger Beer, on the left bank between the main river and the road south from Stockbridge and King's Somborne. Like other Test fishermen, I break my journey a furlong or two from the water at the Bear and Ragged Staff. This is more than a place of refreshment, almost a shrine; an inn where the beer and the welcome are always what they should be.

Fly-fishing is thirsty business, not physically strenuous but not inactive either, and tiring because it demands ceaseless concentration. The sharp tang of malt and hops, enlivening a long-parched gullet, sets in train new ambitions, energies, even inspirations. Not for the first time life begins again at my favourite position, slightly to the right of the dart board. For long I wondered why an inn, at this of all places, bears the name it does. The Bear and Ragged Staff, insignia of the Nevill family, generally refers back to Warwick the Kingmaker, its most distinguished member. What he ever did in the Test valley escaped my reading of history. Hereabouts he is not a folk memory. Instead John o'Gaunt ranks almost as perpetual squire. That earlier operator in the corridors of power owned much land locally. His heirs and successors still do. One of them is the Queen, in Her Majesty's capacity as Duke of Lancaster. I cross some of it in reaching Ginger Beer.

That romantic name applies to a long, wide, slow-moving arm of water, secluded from the public eye and agreeably free from bulls. The sun's angle is still high enough for its rays to strike down into the water, irradiating it and acting as a spotlight on the creatures it contains. There are wonders to behold. Sidling into a position where high reeds camouflage me, I do some practical beholding.

Because its flow is man-controlled, the water here is decelerated, hence more revealing than that of the Itchen. Its surface, unbroken by currents or eddies,

83

does not distort what lies under it. There seems hardly a demarcation between it and the still air of evening, and it is as if the great trout are hovering unsupported above the clean gravel beneath them. Their gills working leisurely, their heads incline from side to side as they watch the travel of approaching flies.

The insects that now fall on the river are in the last stages of their single day of aerial life. Procreation, their prime duty, has been done. Now they are known to us as spinners, from their last aerial dance. In the sunset's level rays, the air is golden with them. They fall, spent and dying on to the water from which they come and the trout rise gently to sip them in. It is an act of care and delicacy, as if of connoisseurs. This is the evening rise, the fly-fisher's holy hour when, if he is good enough, big fish can be taken.

If I am to be good enough, my fishing must be careful and delicate too. It seems impossible that the line which takes out my tiny artificial fly can be made to fall so accurately and so softly that in this utter clarity no fish will detect the counterfeit. But I know from experience that success is possible. I have pulled off my role of confidence trickster in the past and I do so again, twice.

Six for the day. Enough is enough. But it is not quite time to go. This is a magic hour, too magic to be missed. I reel in my line, sit and watch and listen. The shades of night are falling. Swallows and swifts, which throughout the day swerved down the line of the river and ripped the air inches above the water, have gone to roost – the swallows among the rafters of barns, the swifts to their nest sites on church towers or to their own strange sleep, perpetually wheeling on the wing high in the darkened sky. A barn owl passes, pale as a ghost. The plops of trout, snatching at the last falling flies, have become few. The river is nodding off. Even the cries of moorhens, nocturnal as they are, now have a somnolent sound.

The day is truly over. It is time to go. Unseen, unheard, some friends had joined me for the evening rise – two after work on their farms, one from a hospital, and others from their offices in Southampton and Winchester. We stand round our cars, drink a little whisky, and report our doings, tampering only lightly with the truth. Far-away voices and the slam of a door tell that last orders are a thing of the past at the Bear and Ragged Staff.

NEXT morning the first dog rose proclaims harvest only six weeks away, and that the year is turning over. The longest day crowns the season into which a Winter man enters least easily. Mid-summer is an interlude of heat and torpor, of inert air heavy with pollen, the all-pervading sense of fruitfulness invoking satiation rather than zest. Often the daylight hours are more slumberous than the dark as thunder crashes, the sky crackles, and lightning flashes through the velvet summer nights. Too much ease, too little rest; life loses its rhythms.

The longest days bring the shortest nights, and long-drawn evenings end with bats' wings at sundown. The big noctules which, sightless, can hunt beside the swallows, slice downwards through the air and circle the garden, hawking cockchafers and dor beetles, then settle in a pear tree to dismantle and eat them. We hear a ghoulish flapping and gibbering as they drop crunched wing cases on to the lawn, while higher up, speeding to and fro among the midges against the darkening sky, little pipistrelles squeak like airborne mice. How wrong Tennyson was when, in his effort to entice Maud into the garden, he implied that bats are black (an interesting sidelight on that forbidding poet). I have never seen a black bat, though inevitably they appear black when viewed from below. Held in the hand, noctules are chestnut coloured with silky fur, and look much more

85

attractive than they smell, pipistrelles a variegated brown. When dusk has deepened into night hawk moths come out of the blackness, lured by the glow in our windows, their long wings silhouetted against the panes.

With light's last frontiers pushed out towards midnight, and the next daybreak at four o'clock, the respite for animals and birds is brief. The warblers that sing the evening out are swelling the dawn chorus only five hours later. For them and all the others the unrelenting effort of rearing offspring resumes, and starts another nineteen hours' hard labour. Flying out to forage, flying back to stoke up the ever-gaping beaks, a ceaseless shuttle service to keep pace with the nestlings' digestive systems (small wonder that they grow almost visibly), a parent bird's daily life is the point of balance between exhaustion and recuperation.

For mammals, the reverse applies. Most of them feed by night and rest by day. Roe deer and their fawns have only the smallest hours in which to browse, and a full four times as long to wait for the next meal. But now the crops are high, and though the hay is being made most of the corn stands for another two months, packing the fields and turning the countryside into a secret world three feet deep and virtually without lateral limit. In it, under cover of the ripening ears, unseen communities live and travel. Pheasant poults are putting on their feathers, partridge coveys grow up, young rabbits explore the world, saved by the canopy of nodding grain from sighting by hawk or fox, but in constant danger of ambush by stoat or weasel.

In the half dozen weeks after the zenith, Britain has more birds than at any other time of year. Everywhere – in suburbs, fields, woods, hedges and on the moors and mountains – the young have flown their nests. The summer immigrants are still with us. For a time there is gross over-population. We see the sad signs of adjustment on every side, especially on the roads. Wherever fast traffic passes through open country it is rare to find ten yards of road which, in July, does not contain at least one flattened bird carcase. There and elsewhere the natural scavengers – rats, crows and magpies – live richly. The first days of self-reliance are the shake-out time for all wild life, and the rule is survival of the fittest. In most bird species more than half the young of each year die through accident, predation or their own inadequacy in their first week of independent life. Only the strongest and most alert come through.

The combination of short nights and long days gives me one much-prized opportunity. Early dawns extend the period of day-light before the returning human presence. Until the sun burns off the dew there is no point in farmers working in the fields. At least three hours elapse between first light and first men. Then Nature has the country to herself, and all wild creatures enjoy it undisturbed. In these short spells of peace their behaviour is markedly different from that at other times. Little by little I have learned to infiltrate the magic hours without destroying their special harmony.

Once the first stockman has passed by, whistling on his way to work, or the first tractor has approached, or the mail van has sped down the lane, the spell is broken. Until that moment, all the life of the countryside confidently enjoys the peace that afterwards is no longer theirs. Until their moment of unanimous fadeaway on recognising that Man the great intruder is back, there is a Garden of Eden innocence. How to be part of it, but not to break it, is a problem with a simple answer. As I dis-covered years ago, riding out of darkness into light on the way to a cub-hunting meet, it is to go on horseback.

A horse is accepted by wild creatures as just another animal, regardless of the man on his back. When I ride out at a swinging walk between barley fields rolling in shining waves under the breeze of early day, my horse and I pass as a member of their own community. Instead of bolting into the crops baby rabbits sit up, stroking their whiskers and watching unalarmed as we go by, hooves brushing the mid-track weeds within a few yards of them. A little owl on a fence post does not move. A roebuck which would turn his well-adorned backside and decamp were I on foot, stands up after his morning roll and watches me away, instead of me watching him. Hen pheasants sit composedly among their broods.

To them I am just part of the horse, the horse is part of the

87

scene, and a horse is not yet regarded as symptomatic of the human race. But if I were to trot him on, the surroundings would be empty of life in a split second. A horse in a hurry would be out of character with the surrounding tranquillity, and that jarring note would reduce him to the level of intruder, on a par with tractor and mail van. So I carefully observe the distinctions between the functions of a horse; as between, say, a grandstand and a means of acceleration, or an athlete in need of exercise. I push on only where I expect nothing worth seeing.

One day I shall go back, on foot, and take a closer interest in the roebuck. When the first trickles of the drift back to darkness begin to erode the long hours of light, the ceremonies of the ring take place. He may lead me to where they happen.

The shy and graceful roe, our smallest ungulates and among the earliest to be evolved, are the most widely distributed of all deer. The whole northern hemisphere of the Old World is their territory. From Scotland to China and from Siberia to Greece roe deer carry out the same curiously beautiful rites of procreation. First, the belling of the buck – like the voice of a dog which is lost and bewildered – sounds in the far-away darkness when I lie awake with windows wide on a sultry summer night. Generally I hear it first from one bearing, then from another, then receding until lost in the surrounding woods. Only once have I heard the coy little squeal of an answering doe, mistakable for a hedgehog rounding up his family. It is swallowed by the silence in which is hidden what I want to know, which is where their next journey will take them.

When their tryst is made, roebuck and doe go together to one of their ceremonial rings – perhaps miles away in deep woodland, or trodden out on the ling or bracken of an open heath. It may be circular, or in a figure of eight, with diameters of half a dozen yards. It will be worn bare and the soil compacted by the feet of generations of roedeer, dancing there year after year under summer moons. Round and round they go, she leading him on, he complying until enough is enough in their formalisation of pursuit and capture which, in different forms, is the coda before consummation of all warm-blooded life. The dance may last for hours. They will be scrupulous in following the ring's exact outline without short cuts, and they will not leave it until their union is accomplished.

These rings are few and widely scattered. The creation of a new one is a very rare event. Only when mature trees are thrown, temporarily destroying a woodland, is a rutting ring abandoned. Foresters have shown me rings which they have known lifelong, and their fathers before them, where still the roe deer come in pairs, stealing through the shadowed woods. Only one has been found in an eight mile radius of my home, despite a population of hundreds of roe and even though every neighbouring game-keeper knows that a bottle of whisky awaits him who can show me another.

The pilgrimages of roe deer to their rings must lead them across many miles of countryside, after which they return to their own areas. The location of the rings are the framework for roe deer populations. They are so wide apart and limited in number as to be a control against overcrowding – always the hazard against which evolution provides the greatest safeguards for every species except our own. Only there can procreation proceed. The rule of the rings is an iron discipline. We may wonder whether humanity has outgrown such things, or has not learned them yet. Perhaps both.

Meanwhile the roe live on. I sometimes wonder how. They are not innocent of damage to human interests. At the sapling stage,

there are no greater menaces to forestry. Equally there are no
more pitiable victims to persecution; not, be it added, in defence
of forestry or in the course of sport, but in poaching for profit in
the form of export venison to the continent. The main means are
shotguns at night, the use of such weapons on deer being nothing
else than barbarity, and coursing by over-sized lurchers, often
aided by nets. Half-baked politicians and animal-oriented senti-
mentalists, who take pride in sabotaging legitimate hunts which
protect their quarry in its breeding season, and in other ways
ensure its well-being, seldom attack, recognise, or even mention
this brutality. Its perpetrators are beyond reproach by them,
being safely outside the politics of envy.

Crime, of course, is committed by night. Only once, in the
shape of the head and recently gralloched entrails of a doe in
milk, have I found evidence of it in the harmless hours of young
day, when all life seems friendly and dark deeds impossible. Such
flaws as there are on the face of the country seem minor in the
freshness of morning.

To keep the peace, one must do nothing unexpected. Once,
heading home, we inadvertently canter on too far and cause a
major flush of thrushes and blackbirds from the cricket field.
There must be forty of them flying away, their population ex-
plosion as yet unadjusted. It is Saturday, and the outfield was
mown last night, ready for today's match. The birds had been
having a high old time, hopping up and down to cause the vibration which makes worms break surface, then grabbing them
first time from the shaven turf. All very well for the thrushes
and blackbirds. But not, alas, for me.

They no longer pick me now, even as a non-bender. On this
bright day which can lead me on to nothing more glorious than
a deck-chairborne afternoon, I look upon a shrine to lost endea-
vours, the striped field with the table waiting to be chalked, and
muse upon the march of time. They have made me a vice-presi-
dent, which in terms of village cricket protocol is another way of
writing Ichabod. And there are several different significances to
that.

It means that my name will be on the fixture card till death us do part, but never henceforth on the score sheet. Never again will I be asked to pay that vulgarisation of the honest English guinea, £1.05, as my annual subscription; henceforth it will be £5. Never again need I shove and jostle for calling space at the bar; henceforth nobody will usurp my right to buy the first round for all present, and all the other rounds as well if I show the smallest inclination. It is a sign of the times more eloquent than the apparent juvenility of the clergy, the doctor, the policemen and other pillars of society. It signals that a day will come when even the Chelsea Pensioners will seem to be younger than they were.

There are those who set little store by the passage of time; our offspring, for instance. While there is breath in a father's body there are useful outlets into which his energies can be channelled, and Pony Club members are to the fore in exploiting this possibility. I wonder if full employment for paterfamilias may be one of the minor tactics inculcated at some of the lectures which the Pony Club is tireless in organising. The time of year approaches when fathers fall for the press gang in droves. School summer holidays have started; camp, that apex of the pony year, is only days away. My youngest daughter's build-up approaches culmination with that sense of destiny which is beyond the reach of men, but characteristic of women of all ages in matters of total commitment, especially when aided by their mothers. Their objective being defined and accepted, they lock on to it like heat-seeking missiles, attaining it with none of the doubts and susceptibility to distraction to which I, for instance, am liable.

Initially this provides a paternal alibi. It is borne in upon me that all I have to do is write or sanction the appropriate cheques, and stand clear of those with work to do. The work in question includes perfection in turn-out fit for Trooping the Colour, and logistics enough for the Normandy invasion. Articles of furniture, eventually part of several rooms normally devoted to other purposes become dumps for the paraphernalia of Pony Club camp. The process is acoustically fortissimo, psychologically stress-producing, and physically redolent of saddle soap.

The appearance of a dismantled bridle and martingale on the

91

dining table is a sure sign that matters are coming to a head. The bit, buckles and rings gleam with holy lustre. Everything leather has acquired the deep patina which bespeaks elbow grease in polishing. A car has been doing shuttle service to the saddler; the telephone is locked-on to the farrier; jodhpurs, shrunken dramatically, have been replaced in the nick of time; shirts are assembled, the vital tie located. Outside, stable forks and prongs are mobilised in duplicate, and moreover rendered clean, bright and slightly oiled like a guardsman's rifle, if not the guardsman himself. Half the horse-trailer is stacked with hay bales, feed bowls, a sack each of oats and pellets, two water buckets. All that the heart of a pony, or of a District Commissioner, could desire is there. Now there is no longer a day to go; only a night with evening shadows falling. The clocks tick on. Tomorrow will be a race with time.

"We'll be all right," my wife says, "if only you can get me out of bed in time."

Confident of being able to do that small thing, I give my promise. Not having yet learned all life's lessons, I add, "Anything else I can do to help in any way?" and receive the disarming answer, "It would be lovely if you would help us load the car and trailer." Experienced fathers will know that thereby I have sold my soul, and my body. Concerned only to indicate general goodwill, team spirit and parental support, I am integrated into the team, though I do not know it yet. Of course I shall not be the only victim.

Next morning the truth emerges. In its small way, this is Crispin's day. Who am I to be one of those gentlemen of England, fast a'breakfast if not fast abed, when their daughters are off to Pony Club camp. So I am still aboard when car and trailer leave, springs flattened, for the racecourse stables where camp is being held. What is more, I have a near miss from the driving seat, which should be avoided by every prudent father on this particular journey. To drive away is natural, but to be driving on arrival is disastrous. There is a serious risk that the trailer will have to be reversed tortuously into a confined space, and a father who cannot accomplish this feat with due insouciance will

be a source of embarrassment to his progeny. The sight of him revving, braking, coming out again, making repeated attempts at what ought to be easy, and all in full view of other campers and their sires and dams, is enough to bring a blush to the cheek of any damsel. In my opinion, this is woman's work which most of them are proud to do, and hence should be allowed to get on with. There is good cause for this. Experienced Pony Club mothers have much practice, and would be undaunted by the problem of the camel and the needle's eye.

My expectations are fulfilled. The trailer is safely inserted into a space only inches larger than itself, and a cohort of fathers are already in action. Like the porters on Mount Everest, we are humping and stockpiling on behalf of those destined for higher things. We heave and stack fodder and what goes with it, convey suitcases, remember where everything is, and marvel inwardly at the enormous force of femininity, here where all minds have but a single thought.

At first this is expressed in mutual admiration, not of each other but of their ponies. As each is led up to pass the vet, every eye is upon it; eyes which have in them the star-crossed look of those who have entered a separate existence, as if the souls behind them had withdrawn from this terrestrial plane and entered another peopled only by themselves. Speak to our daughter now, and could we count on being recognised? They alone are instantly their own reality.

Any mystery there may ever have been about the role of Juno in the Pony Club is dispersed by this graphic, even daunting evidence. He would be a bold male who intruded here. To check if any have, I consult the nominal roll pinned on the board outside the Weighing Room, now doing duty as headquarters. To my surprise a David, a Roddy, a Hugh and several more are listed. They are not visible yet, but they have my admiration. At a quick computation they are outnumbered nine to one by girls. The time will come when some will find the ratio enviable. Now I marvel at their nerve as we drive away, speculating on their survival plans for the next week.

At home, the tumult and the shouting are suddenly memories.

Never mind what happens on dune and headland, here peace descends, akin to a vesper calm. We pour drinks, and enjoy them. The enjoyment is the greater for not being ours alone. Life must have its golden hours, especially for those growing up, and the Pony Club is unexcelled in providing them.

SOON afterwards we set off on a journey. August is the month for Scotland, and going there, no matter how often, is a major pilgrimage. Though no drop of Scottish blood dilutes the English in me, the prospect of crossing the Border still stirs feelings of anticipation and a sense of occasion. I have wondered much why this should be. Mine has not been a static life. I have trotted the globe, seeing new things and places, being one of those, along with Kipling's tramp, and the gipsies on the down, who "must get hence, and go observing matters". To travel is nothing new to me. But the annual sojourn in Scotland is separate from this wanderlust, and transcends it, by conferring its own presentiment.

Perhaps the explanation lies in the plain fact of North. My time in southern hemisphere has been brief, so I do not know whether people in New Zealand, Argentina or Chile feel a comparable attraction towards their nearer Pole. But I do not doubt that in the northern hemisphere's New World as well as in the Old, the call of the North comes compellingly to too many people for its strange power to be denied. It may stem from something deep and elemental in the human psyche, perhaps related to the magnetic pole as well as to the geographic one. Not only in our islands but in Scandinavia and North America too, men turn their hearts and minds to the North when their spirits need refreshment by challenge. They are certainly in that sense magnetised, and magnetism could take other forms.

That this attraction should be felt especially, possibly solely, by us whose life quickens when out of doors does not surprise me. We are naturally the more likely to respond to an influence which originates in Nature; a response which could be expected to atrophy in others whom circumstance or preference insulates from Nature's touch and calls. We North-goers seek different objectives from those going South, as the travel pages of any newspaper make clear. We are not looking for soft options. They are. Like the moths on the window panes, they are seekers of heat and light.

For them ease is the essence of the contract, warmth an important subsidiary, sunshine the currency, food and drink basic interests. Scotland does not offer ease to those who leave the roads behind them, but demands much exertion; warmth is irrelevant there, sunshine no more than intermittent for most of the time, even in summer; and though it would be a most unusual Scottish situation in which thirst became a problem, one eats to live there, rather than living to eat.

From the blunt, rounded hills of Wessex to the glens beyond the Cairngorms, the distance is six hundred miles. They can be flown in a few hours, but not by those travelling with rods and guns, dogs and kit to last for four rough weeks. Trains lift cars and passengers across them in a night, a blessedly unconscious journey. The miracle of reading oneself to sleep in the English Midlands and lifting the blind on to a view of great fir trees once part of the ancient Caledonian forest round Aviemore is well worth experiencing – but not too often at the price now charged for it. For me the road has become the only way, if also the hard way. There is an ancient tradition of taking the high road or the low road to Scotland, though the distinction has long been blurred. The road we take is thronged and raucous in the South, busy until the Forth is crossed, then merging by stages into the solitudes which are Scotland's peace. Two hours at sixty-miles-an-hour bring us off our own chalk hills, through the racehorse country, across the infant Thames, over the Cotswolds and up the M5 to the first halt, with the great whale shape of the Malvern Hill away to the West. Then we raise the pace up the motorway, flanked at first by Shakespeare's England, round leafy Birmingham (at least it looks leafy from the elevated road which threads its suburbs), linking with M6 in the chemicals belt, where the air-intakes suck in an atmosphere like an ill-ventilated laboratory, and past the service area at Hilton where in my youth I rode to meets on what is now the north-bound car park. Rural Staffordshire, ever-fresh with rolling farms and winding brooks, gives the off-watch co-driver a fair view until Cheshire supervenes, speckled with Friesian herds.

We stop again to change drivers, and eat a picnic lunch. The M6 service areas are good, but some on other routes are squalid, and I have learned which to avoid. There are better places, generally transport cafes sited off-motorway but near to intersections, and well known to the prosperous cosmopolitans who drive juggernauts to and from the Common Market. They are accustomed to better things than queue-jammed, paper-littered cafeterias, and so am I. So for years I have joined them, and now know my way around England via a network of those more agreeable refuges which, offering no frills, provide excellent food, good company, and almost every European language among the all-male clientele. Though I do not believe that I pass for one of the brotherhood, nobody has ever hinted by word or look that perhaps I should be somewhere else. However, they are scarcely family resorts, and on this trip the conventions are followed.

We tank-up, drive on, and join the thickening pressure of industrial heavyweights conserving their kinetic downhill energy as they head for Lancashire. The big black steeplechase fences of Haydock show fleetingly on the right, one of the courses which bring out greatness in a racehorse. The smell of the outer world is hot and oily hereabouts, the traffic ever more dense. The destination boards at the frequent exits read like the Football League. Here I learn where Accrington, Bury and Tranmere are, giving substance to names that were formerly the stuff of dreams. The landscape for a time looks hot and drab, layered by cloud under which purposeful kits of pigeons fly; racing birds on training flights, distinguished even at long distance by their precision and sharp wing beats from the woodpigeons which, in very different circumstances, I watched across a winter sky.

Abruptly, the scene clears. An intersection, now behind us, has deflected many heavy vehicles towards the Manchester-Liverpool conurbations, and along the East Lancashire road. The countryside is green again as M6 leads pleasantly on, swinging round hillsides, under graceful bridges, over Ribble and Lune, salmon rivers which are an earnest of what is to come. The day is wearing on, the air cooler as we begin the long ascent of Shap, up dark hills on which the cotton grass has faded, past the lonely railway settlement of Tebay, and a hummock in the heather which is all that is left of a butt where I shot grouse in pre-motorway days. So to Britain's most hard-won summit of the past. Cars now take without difficulty what must in coaching days have been a hell for horses, and in recent memory a challenge for railmen who could couple and uncouple the great steam locomotives which, as second engines, helped to haul the night expresses over, without awakening those who slept along the train.

The height that we were slow to gain is only slowly lost. Ahead the land is bright, green pastures replacing the dull fogg of the moors behind. The road sinks to the wide vale of Eden, well named, and across the flats to Gretna Green, haven of lovers long ago. After that we turn off the main road, first into a lane, then by ever smaller tracks, and over a humped bridge to a farmhouse for the night.

Coming to familiar places, the eye takes in the changes, and the samenesses. The lanes seem more narrow this time, because their banks have not been trimmed, indicating a Region short of ratepayers' money; small wonder, ratepayers being few. Beside the tracks some calves are grazing, which means the farmer has gone out of pigs since last year, though he has left the pig-wire up. In such ways is memory re-activated by scenes long dor-

mant, but now alive again. On the bridge a youth
sits stationary on a racing bicycle, one foot on
the ground. His free hand holds a fly-rod, so in
silhouette against the setting sun he suggests a
lancer ready for action. His eyes are on the burn
below, which rollicks along over a stoney bed,
its edges lost under trailing loosestrife.

He is Jamie from the next farm up. We stop
beside him. I tell him I shall be back in twenty
minutes, to catch my breakfast; which side of the
bridge will he be fishing?

"Och, there's watter enoo," he answers, "and
aye troot, lots o' pan-sizers."

Only twenty miles into Scotland, and
England is a whole nation behind. The words,
their intonation, are as Scottish as if we had
sighted Perth. Already we are in easy-go, share-alike country
where troot are troot and only salmon are fush. The Sassenach
in me lowers its profile as we drive up to the farm.

Light is softening across the white-walled yard. The air is cool,
fresh and free from oil reek and scorching tyres. The homely
smell of hay and dung and beasts and nearby flowers, hot from
a long day, tune our senses to a country evening. Conversations
begun eleven months previously are resumed as if never interrupted. I drink a cup of tea, give the dogs five minutes' leg-
stretch, pick up the rod loaded free for the purpose, and walk
back to the burn, assembling it as I go. Jamie has merged into
the background. Then I see him, half-crouching, one knee on a
flat stone, gazing at something worth watching. He has left me
all Scotland above the bridge. So I walk upstream, my eyes to
the North.

From here I can see no habitation, and few signs of human
handiwork. A few stone dykes stretch over the skyline far away,
dividing one sheep walk from another, and on a distant tawny
hill a fank bears witness that even so there is sorting out to do
when flocks become mixed. Apart from those who own it, shepherds are the ruling class on these wind-swept expanses, each a

supreme being as he rides his thousands of acres on a tough Dales pony, or even a thoroughbred retired from the Turf; they know their horses in the Cheviots. When the Hunts come, out for the big hill foxes which are death to any lamb they meet, the shepherd by custom rides with them until they have left "his" hill, part in mutual respect, part to keep an eye on what the hounds do.

The burn flows from the great tract of Eskdalemuir, where the air is liquid with the voices of redshank and golden plover. Beyond the muir, and East and West of it, the Cheviots stretch wide and far, and depopulated of all life save sheep and birds, linking other Border hills until the Lowlands are reached. Most of us think of the far North as Scotland's empty quarter, forgetting that here, flanking the Border, is Britain's greatest expanse of unpopulated country where hardy men live their lives under the inspiration of its beauty, defiant of its distances, its weather, and its hidden hazards. So it has been through history. Only half a dozen roads cross it South to North. In four counties – Peebles, Selkirk, Roxburgh and Berwick, stretching from the North Sea to Solway Firth – there is no town large enough to rank more than a village in England, and few enough of those. The stark hills, 2,000 feet high, are tawny with bracken or dark with heather, treacherous with swamps, and laced with plunging streams.

Like the Welsh March, this tract where two nations meet bears its past in its place names. With landmarks like Bloodybush Edge, Watchman Hill, Black Dod (the word means death) as reminders, it does not need telling that this was reiver country where most men lived by spilling blood until somebody spilled theirs. Fugitives from justice and from blood feuds, army deserters, political runaways from the powers to North and South, adventurers and plain bad hats made this their home country. From the time when the Picts swept down on the Roman wall to the days of the Covenanters and then Bonnie Prince Charlie, this was country in which to keep one's head down and only fools asked questions. Not far North from where I stand rod in hand is the steep-sided hole in the hills which men still call the

Devil's Beef Tub, where the rustlers shared the spoil after raids
on English cattle. In this now tranquil scene tempestuous centuries passed in which one never knew who might next be met.
Some moss-troopers looked misleadingly respectable. Witness
the brief conversation between Sir Walter Scott's lady of quality
and a man of mettle on Brignall Bank. In my mind I hear them
speaking as I stand there, watching for a moving trout.

> 'With burnished brand and musketoon
> So gallantly you come,
> I read you for a bold dragoon
> That lists the tuck of drum.'

> 'I list no more the tuck of drum,
> No more the trumpet hear;
> But when the beetle sounds his hum
> My comrades take the spear.'

In the surrounding immensity, small wonder hearts were
stirred and sometimes lost elsewhere than Gretna Green. The
establishment and the mobsters met and went their ways in that
labyrinth where the law was a laughing matter. Back in the
present, the evening wind comes down the stream, blowing from
where we are going. It all seems very innocent now. But just as
there is nothing new under the sun, so also nothing ever happens
for the last time. A heifer tramples up and stands behind me as
I reel in a fish, blowing her sweet breath into my ear, a gentle
beast in, at this moment, a gentle scene. But I wonder, and
wonder again. The lesson of life is that we have seen it all before,
so somebody will see it all again. By the time my nearest beetle
sounds his hum I have caught breakfast for us all.

Sun up and still far to go, we take the road next day, familiar
landmarks ahead. With trout fried in oatmeal inside us, we now
eat the miles. Beattock Summit and Red Moss come and go. In
a heat haze half-left lies Glasgow, no mean city full of sterling
men, but fallen on hard times. Our route runs right-handed here,

eastward towards the clipped vowels and refinements of Edin-
burgh; turning short of the capital, we cross the Forth at Kin-
cardine Bridge.

So much glamour attaches to the Highlands (perhaps another
function of the "North" syndrome) that the Lowlands are often
thought second-class Scotland. It is bad misjudgment. Still bor-
rowing a bit of East, we leave the Kilsyth, Fintry and Ochil hills
on our left, every Scottish route being a low road for choice. All
the way the solid worth of Scottish land and Scots people shows
up as plainly as in more publicised areas. The land is rich. No
better soil exists in all Britain; gutty stuff, a bit heavy perhaps,
but tamed by tillage over centuries. The crops look good. Farmers make few mistakes up here, leave nothing undone, and the
harder northern climate reduces the insect pests. Big, substantial
farmhouses tell the story; well-found villages and cottar houses
confirm it. Down Glenfarg, where the new road lifts the average
speed, we see the first heather flowering, the Summer purple
instead of the umber of the rest of the year.

This is the other face of Scotland. Heather is to Scots what
sand is to Arabs, an element into which to retreat. In heather,
withdrawn into the endless miles and trackless wastes of it, the
soul of Scotland has found security in which to fan the flames of
ancient faiths and romances. The warm unity of a small nation,
the hospitality born of generations who shared the slender resources of a hard country in hard times, the call made on manhood and self-reliance by rugged backgrounds and a stern climate, have made the nation confident, resourceful, tough.

With the Tay behind us, and Sidlaw's hills now on the left,
the hand-prints of man on Scotland change as the miles pass.
Stateliness and prosperity mark the baronial counties of Angus
and Aberdeen, the latter approached by Cairn o'Mounth to
side-step the granite city itself. The high life is left behind us in
the straths of Dee and Don, and we cross into the lost and lonely
Cabrach, a kind of misplaced tundra, where survival is the name
of the game, and to be snowed-in a way of life. It is an environment which hones the human qualities and, weather permitting,
induces a keen desire for conviviality.

Small stone crofts, low-built and dug-in to lie under the ever-lasting winds, dot the bare landscape below the line of heather and granite outcrop. Inbye fields of oats and barley, defended by dry-stone dykes against the encroaching wild, may be harvested by November, perhaps never. Whole families, from bairns to grannies, are bringing in the hay. Some crofts share balers, most of which have seen better days. On others, the lifting and carrying has changed little since Macbeth; the sled, the pony pack saddle, the strong human back. The ricks which it makes are small and round, as they are also in Wales and Ireland, Cornwall and Brittany, wherever the local folk are Celt-descended; rectangular ricks proclaim Saxons. When built and topped they are anchored by rope-linked boulders, lest a gale overturns them, literally blowing to the winds not only a whole summer's work but a whole winter's feed for the croft's stock.

The Cabrach is something between a vast bowl and a vast sponge. Some of the burns which thread across it, down from the peat and heather, between the rare patches of cultivatable ground, flow on to the almost sacred Highland edifices, distilleries producing world-famous whisky. Others unite to form the Deveron, an exciting salmon river reputed to yield fish to only those anglers born and bred in Banffshire. We have proved this an exaggeration, but to do so is a hard struggle. Otherwise only five forms of non-human life defy the elements here – grouse and deer on the high moors, sheep and beef stots lower down, and rabbits everywhere. This haunted place, this savage place, is peopled by families who, when most folk seek soft living, are united in a single indestructible conviction. Nowhere on this planet would life be supportable for them except in the Cabrach.

We stop the car in a lay-by carved from a braeside, less a passing place than a refuge from blizzard. The wind is such as we have not felt since last we stood here for a farewell view. It comes to us off the northern sea, across twenty open miles, singing through bents and rushes, whistling round a rocky bluff. We take those first ceremonial breaths of braeside air by which a man inhales Scotland and thereby becomes, for the duration, a different being; we ease cramped muscles for five minutes. This is enough. They will have seen us, those of keen eye in crofts a mile and more away on a **45°** arc, and they will pass the word around. We shall not be unexpected when we pay our first calls. We drive on. The last lap is soon accomplished.

Northern evenings stretch late. By the length of daylight, it might still be mid-summer here. Bathed, changed and civilised, we take our drams on to the terrace and drink in not only them, but the view across the Moray Firth, a scene of far tranquillity. The sun is going down over the Black Isle. The sea darkens towards violet. A slow mist is rising. Above it, fifty miles off, purple shadows gather at the foot of Morven, most graceful of the Sutherland peaks. The wind which has blown all day drops with evening, but the light does not drain away here as soon as the sun has gone. The sky plays out time in northern purity, fading from amethyst to aquamarine, then paling to neutrality as the lighthouses begin to stab the gathering darkness.

Only six hundred miles, yet a different world. In prospect the journey had seemed a long one, but only because the smallness of our island governs our scale of overland distances. On the face of Canada or Australia it would have been insignificant, the country at one end of it no change from the other. Yet the breadth of contrast between Wessex and Scotland cannot be gainsaid.

What can one say of Scotland to explain its compulsive attraction for people from the South? Nothing which adds up to a coherent explanation. All I can do is to offer a few vignettes. The chords they strike in other people may lead some of us a little nearer to the truth.

A Walk at Evening

ON this first evening, at last light, I walk down the drive and
along an empty road. No longer am I looking out to sea,
but focussing on the flowers at my feet in the Scottish application of that phrase, renewing acquaintance with friends of former
years. Round a certain bend I find a tall whin bush spectacularly
snaggle-headed; further on a mass of mare's tail left over from
the Ice Age, a clump of wild raspberries, and a drift of rosebay
blood-red at the end of the day. These small reminders confirm
where I am, easing my transition into the Scottish way of life.

When I step off the road and onto its rough and hummocky
verge, the hard crust of Scotland under foot comes as an annual
shock. I am accustomed to going cross-country but now I feel a
tenderfoot. To turn an ankle over at home is a rare mishap, here
very easy. The brick-like composition of hard-baked Scottish
soil, the intermingled rock, the steep gradients prove the com-
parative softness of the South. Yet in a single day wind and limb
will be tuned-in and I shall walk a moor as well as anybody else,
for as long as anybody else, and without noticeable effort. Scotland upgrades us all.

These encouraging reflections are interrupted by a sound now
unknown in most of England. A corncrake is calling in the half-
dark, as corncrakes often do, and in full darkness also. The
double rasp goes on and on with maddening irregular pauses. It
persists, like the coppersmith bird of the Indian plains, until it
dominates the mind. The suspense of waiting for the next break,
and the frustration of trying in vain to anticipate when it will
come, deaden all other thoughts.

People who remember corncrakes in England, which I do not,
deplore their loss from the sound-track of country evenings.
Listening to this one's contribution to the peaceful northern
twilight, I doubt if life would be much improved by my hearing
it at home. Inevitably we regret every cessation, the loss of any
species, the absence of any voice once part of our forefathers'
memories. But corncrakes, seldom seen even where most often
heard, seem no great loss. They obviously pass through England
in fair numbers twice each year, on passage North to Scotland,
especially the Hebrides, in Spring, and on return in Autumn.

105

Yet they are seldom noticed, even though their flight, somewhat ineffective and seldom long sustained, would seem to give plenty of opportunity.

The name mystifies me, the bird being unquestionably a crake, but the association with corn not apparent. This one is calling from what can well be described as a blasted heath, where scrub willow was torn out to make way for cultivation abandoned when an expected grant was not forthcoming. I have never heard them call from cornfields. Farming, other than by making the best use of waste land, cannot be blamed for their disappearance from England. Tonight, far North in Scotland on a coast with no land between it and the polar ice, the voice of the corncake follows me home.

Jutting eastward from Scotland's central mountains, the land mass of Buchan ("the bulge") is a region which has inherited whatever is most elemental and most varied in Scottishness. Much of the world's best whisky is made here, the amount drunk locally being impressive. This results from a fertile soil and a foul climate, the former producing the wherewithal and the latter the reason for a regular intake of drams.

The Cairngorm range is a barrier to soft airstreams from the South, so the main weather influences come either from or across the Moray Firth, of which Buchan is the southern shore. This long coastline, West to East all the way from Inverness to Fraserburgh, takes the first brunt of anything coming out of the North, against which it has no defence. Nothing from that quarter is likely to be welcome, either in itself, or in the effect it has in stirring up the Firth. This wide arm of the sea is not only tempestuous, but very cold. Not a teaspoonful of Gulf Stream water enters it. Hence the striking difference between the West coast of Scotland, lushly vegetated and dotted with superb gardens because it is warmed by the Stream and defended by the Hebrides, and the uncompromising harsh bareness of the East. Having swum in the Firth annually for years, I can testify. So can science. Because of that much under-rated current from the Caribbean, the sea is warmer at Tromso, where it meets the coast of Norway nearly 300 miles inside the Arctic Circle, than in the Moray Firth.

On a day of sunshine, clear skies, and air like wine we sail across it on a north-west heading to the Sutherland coast, watching the mountains grow taller out of the sea. The voyage back gives a panoramic view of Buchan's bold front to the storms. Little ports, sea-walled like fortresses and clinging limpet-like below cliffs of granite and marble, are lined across our front from port to starboard – Rosehearty, MacDuff, Banff, Portsoy, Portknockie, Findochty, Buckie, Lossiemouth, Burghead – they are unknown or forgotten elsewhere until a trawler (not necessarily one of ours) signals distress. Then theirs are the names of salvation behind stout sea defences while gales howl outside, the whole northern ocean surges in, and breakers pound on our island's most assaulted front. In all of them men saved from the sea, and with cause to know the old enemy all too well, have thanked God with equal fervour in kirk and pub for the help of Buchan men.

On our calm day, reaching for home, a passing view of Dornoch Firth to Strath Oykel reminded me of another day, long since in the past. In hard Spring weather I was helping a moor keeper to count grouse nests. All day we walked a deer track westward up that wide, wind-eroded valley, Ben More Assynt on our right, Easter Ross to the left, with English setters ranging out to point sitting birds on either side, giving evidence of their density. A man can stretch his eyes there, as well as his legs. The scene is much as the last glacier of the Ice Age left it. In the desolation small things show up miles ahead. At mid-morning a dark dot broke the pattern miles away. Half an hour later it was larger, evidently not stationary, probably moving head-on to us. In another half hour it was indisputably a human figure, striding purposefully along the same contour as ourselves. Ten more minutes, and he was on the same deer track, which was only inches wide but guaranteed sound footing all the way.

Another five and the figure was male, burly, hatless, thick dark hair blowing in the wind, clad in a dark blue donkey jacket, and, strangely in that setting, not carrying a long stick to give balance over heather. I, ahead of the keeper, continued steady on course. He came purposefully towards me, eyes down, pre-occupied, abstracted. Collision threatened. We had been in each other's sight for more than an hour. There had been nothing else to see. He must have known that I was there, in front of him. Somebody had to give way. I stepped a yard into the heather. He passed without word, gesture, glance, or change of pace.

Even so we had almost rubbed shoulders. I saw that he was unshaven. The expectations built up across an hour and a quarter, and perhaps seven miles of empty landscape, vanished in an instant of non-contact and left an anti-climax. He passed the keeper similarly. We turned and stood watching him stride on, as though Kyle of Sutherland, all that lay ahead, was the object of a pilgrimage, and nothing else mattered.

"A Harris man," said the keeper, as if that explained everything.

The small things that, for no reason, mark one's life do not fade with time. Years have passed since that sombre man and I had met, passed so closely, and gone our ways. Yet when, from the yacht's deck, I have my fleeting view towards the scene of it, it is of him that I think, not of the many others whom I knew better, and for longer, with whom I shared times worth remembering in and around that place. Questions, some profound, some banal, recur. Did he have a secret sorrow that made him oblivious to all else? I recalled his sullen face. Or just a major hangover? How far had he walked across that otherwise trackless waste? Not less than eight miles before I first saw him; and what man who knows heather goes so far without a stick? Why had he chosen to walk the track? Why had he not walked the road, parallel and less than a mile away, and given himself the near-certainty of the lift seldom refused in that stark zone? How had the keeper known that he was a Harris man? Do all men of Harris go through life taciturn, ignoring others? To my knowledge I have never met another Harris man, though I have a friend who is a Lewis man, and he is talkative enough. Whence had this one started his long lonely walk? Presumably at Ullapool, where the island steamers berth. It was a long way to have come. And where, now, has he gone. We two met momentarily in the presence of a third, with no other soul within miles. The mark he made on me is with me yet. Has he forgotten me?

Land-based again in Buchan I meet old friends. When they have recalibrated their dialect so that I can understand it, we span the year's separation. A shepherd, two ghillies, a grieve and a bee-master make up a school at a village clachan. We drink beer and whisky chasers, and eat pickled eggs to keep us upright. This is a well-recommended diet in Buchan, the evening counterpart of porridge for most except kirk elders. It adds nothing to the clarity of the language.

Scottish speech is comparable to that of India, where sixteen major languages have more than five hundred distinctive local variations, all mutually incomprehensible, and in the Orwellian manner some more incomprehensible than others. In Scotland "the Buchan" is the peak of incomprehensibility, sometimes to other Buchan-speakers.

The grieve (in England, farm manager) is a case in point. Though a model of lucidity on home ground, he is in serious difficulty if he has to buy cigarettes in the small town four miles away. His outlandish diction reduces the shop assistants there to giggles, and him to embarrassment. This reflects the pattern of Scottish rural life in pre-motoring days, still just within living memory of oldsters in these latitudes. Its structure centred on the farm-towns where the mains (the big house) was surrounded by the cottar-houses of the workers, and was also the focal point for shepherds, crofters, ghillies and moor keepers on the periphery. Each such small community lived most of the year exclusively in their own company, isolated from towns, villages and other outside contact by work in summer and weather in winter. Families were the basic units, and the families were knit together in interdependence regardless of wealth or class. From sunrise to sunset they worked the land in the hasteless Scottish way –

everybody helping, nobody idling, and nobody hurrying either. When winter came the necessities for life had been laid by. For all but the wealthy, they were simple; the meal sack, the tattie heap, the well, the cupboard for luxuries, the goatie for milk, the turf stack for warmth, and the keg for the water of life. It was enough to last from October into May, during which months snow might cut off a farm-town at any time for weeks at a stretch.

In each such enclosed community the folk spoke seldom to anybody except each other, developing ears and tongues for their own inflections, accents and idioms so that to outsiders they would seem to speak in private codes. Times have changed, but this esoteric speech, the family unit, the keg, and life's gentle pace survive into our easier age as symbols of past days. Since "the oil," cottar houses are centrally heated; their rooms are bright, comfortable and dominated by expansive television screens, whence comes the language of the world beyond. Young people travel out each day to jobs at a distance, so wealth and sophistication flow back, and I am the outsider now – groping to catch a shred of meaning from the quick-bandied parlance of Buchan, as baffling a patois as I have met anywhere on the globe.

A local minister explained it to me. He is a piskie (local term for a clergyman who endangers his soul by having truck with bishops), so has a wider and more objective view than most. He tells me that Buchan is the product of five linguistic roots. Its syntax and part vocabulary are Gaelic. To this, Norse and German words have been added by fishing boat crews from across the North Sea who use the Firth ports. A greater influx of French dates back to the Auld Alliance. And somewhere along the line a number of English words and expressions have crept in. The resultant melange lends a tincture of mystery to a conversation continuing far into the night with only each tenth word recognisable, or thereabouts.

The ghillies hold a dirge-like conclave about the misfortunes of their craft, lamenting equally the dearth of salmon and of gentlemen, the latter a species apparently approaching extinction. They openly cite me as the only specimen to cross their path in months. I take the hint and buy yet another round. The bee-master, who deploys forty hives here and there, scooping up honey from the heather, deplores with the shepherd the influence on the moors of the like of the ghillies. The grieve confronts the rest of us with an air of dignified resignation – a sign, they say, that he is pleuchered. The liquor combines with the talk's sing-song pulse to make us all feel sleepy, but nobody is so weak-kneed as to suggest going home. Then there is an unparliamentary undertone, syllables are rapped out faster and faster until they explode like pistol shots. Money is flung on a table. The grieve undergoes an attack of self-importance. It seems that a bet has been struck. In the nick of time we make for the door. The landlady utters curses upon us, on all others who have stopped spending, and especially on me for leading simple men astray. She says everything except double-double toil and trouble. The landlord is not in evidence, and nobody is surprised. We file out, immersing ourselves in that dangerous element, fresh air. There is much handshaking, many exchanges of cordial wishes for the future. The homing instinct does not fail. It has been an affa guid wee crack-and-speering in the Buchan.

ROUND us, in immensity remarkable for a small country, lies the heather, which Scots refer to, generically, as "the hill". It is a many-sided concept, much more than merely botanical, or topographical, or sporting. As the Border country shows, it is, among other things, another world. Into its trackless distances its convoluted glens and corries, men have been absorbed to keep trysts, dodge pursuit, and to remain alive when others would wish them otherwise. On the blunt-topped ridge at which I look, a survivor from Culloden outfoxed the English redcoats for three years, refusing to leave the heather, dodging them in and out of caves and screes and peat hags, until they gave him best and went home. His descendants still own that landscape. Even today a man could pass from Hadrian's Wall to Cape Wrath, all but a dozen or so miles on heather, never going along roads, emerging into the public eye only when crossing one.

The heather is monochrome for most of the year, but a blaze of glory in late summer. It is that timeless, spaceless thing, wilderness. Into wilderness better men than I have withdrawn to replenish their inner fires since time immemorial. It is a background for the hopes and fears of those who did just that. Bruce and the spider, the fugitive Wallace, the prince who went over the water, and countless thousands who left no mark on history, only on the scene they left. Tap o'Noth, for instance, where men hauled hundreds of tons of stone up precipice slopes to build a fort high above the surrounding prehistoric country. Wind and weather would long since have disintegrated it and flung it back into the glen below but for one strange circumstance. At some time the unmortared walls were seared by flames so hot that the stones melted and when they cooled, fused solidly together, immoveable for ever.

The mystery remains. Did those who built the fort fire the walls intentionally so that, by vitrifying them, they made them indestructible? Or did besiegers, trying to burn out the garrison, melt them incidentally? The fire could not have been an accident. It must have involved labour comparable to the building of the fort itself. We cannot guess the truth, but we can picture the possibilities. In the mind's eye this secluded patch of rock and

112

heather reverts to a savage place. Toiling men in hundreds gasp and curse. Stone by stone, hoisted by ant-like effort, the ramparts and the apron take shape. The endless Highland wind blows in freshly, and blows away rancid with human sweat and the reek of the raw pelts which are the toilers' only clothes. What will, or what terror, drives them on, posterity will never know. The peril is theirs alone. But even these remote forerunners showed a thoroughly Scottish trait. What they set out to do, they did; and were not daunted by what seems impossible today until at last the dried dead whins, collected from miles around, racked and stacked in masses on the near-vertical slopes below, went up in a roaring white-heat holocaust driven over the fort by some unpitying northern gale.

Whether it was triumph or disaster, whether the builders of the fort cheered for joy or were fried alive, the folk of the quiet village of Rynie still point to Tap o'Noth, high on their skyline, to tourists who look up in wonder. Even from twenty miles away, it is different from everything around it. To me, close at hand, it needs no telling that something awesome happened here. I feel the skin behind my neck contract, a sense of chill, and of fellow feeling sparked by memory. I do not forget Kohima Hill. So when waiting for grouse to come, I keep my back to Tap o'Noth. It is a time to enjoy and Tap o'Noth belongs to the grim side of the heather, like that dark cleft that is Glencoe, the menacing water of Lochindorb and empty Culloden where the clans abandoned hope.

But today is all light. I am watching up-sun towards Brux, the skyline beyond which lies another surviving patch of the old forest which from the Middle Ages until Stuart times covered most of Scotland. There the ancient trees are well spaced out after swaying to the storms of centuries, letting the sunshine through to the ground around them. The combination of cover, shelter and air space well suits the capercaillie (Gaelic for cock of the woods), turkey-sized cousins of the grouse. Despite their size and apparent airborne clumsiness, they fly deceptively fast, as non-locals who try to shoot them soon discover. They have never been on my agenda; nor, now, will they ever be.

113

Here and there all over that wide vista, grouse coveys are lying unseen. I hear their voices, "Go-back, Go-back". They are just as likely to be unseen when they are not lying, but flying. Grouse are the best camouflaged of all game birds, in the air or on the ground. They are heather coloured, and invisible against its background except to trained eyes actually looking for them. We are not looking yet. The Buck, the crag-topped summit to the South, rears against the sky. The open Cabrach, rightwards and below, is full of sunshine. White crofts, scattered miles apart, are basking in it. The whole scene smiles instead of scowling. My mind wanders, one of the fringe benefits of grouse shooting. In the sun's warmth, bees come and go. I can hear them on all sides, their buzzing sharp-edged by a sense of purpose. Perhaps they are gathering for one of the bee-master's forty colonies. If each hive contains thirty thousand bees (a low estimate) he must have a million and a quarter working for him. A solemn thought, quite enough to send him to the clachan of an evening. Flies discover me; gross, shiny, with green backsides, they represent the unacceptable face of Nature. There must be almost as many flies as bees. I wonder what they are doing here, on what they live, how they occupy themselves during the **355** days of the year when there are no grouse-shooters to pester. It is a fact that wherever there are grouse-shooters, flies are also present. There is a story of an elderly grouse-shooter to whom the flask meant much. On an afternoon when nobody else fired a shot, he kept up a lively fusillade, lead spouting from his butt as fast as he could reload. But there were no birds to pick up when all was over. He had been bombarding bluebottles at the end of his gun barrels, under the impression that they were grouse coming over, sixty yards out.

Seen against the sky, that is precisely how grouse appear, small swinging dots. When the view from the butt is towards a crest, or downwards on to heather, the dots are more difficult to pick up, their line of approach more misleading. At eighty yards it seems that they might be going anywhere; then, all in an instant, they come in direct, head-high as if a multiple bumper had been bowled at cricket. Suddenly their red eye-patches can be seen, the sign that they are in shot. Just as suddenly, they are over and gone. That is how it will be.

Perhaps surprisingly, I have shot better at grouse than at other game, supposedly easier. I do not believe that any game is in truth easier. All game species provide their own problems – the concealed speed of pheasants, the surprise element and aerial swerve of partridges. It is not grouse, but grouse-shooting, which has favoured me. Its tempo permits the relaxed concentration, and synchronisation of eye and hand. At partridges and pheasants the participants are in full view of each other, perhaps chatting until action impends, denying themselves the chance to settle down. On a grouse moor an hour may pass in which something or nothing may happen; if, as generally happens, it is nothing, that time goes by in solitude but not with inattention as coming events take shape. Success in any endeavour, of which sport is only a sample, requires this element isolation. It may be actual isolation in the sense of being apart from others, or simply isolation of the spirit. My isolation at a grouse drive is counterpart to that of the golfer around whom the gallery freezes for a crucial putt, the snooker player cocooned in concentration while marshalling his whole self into preparation for a crucial stroke, those batsmen round whom there fell a breathless hush in the close one night.

Individual performance is the antithesis of team effort. For it one must be unconscious of all others. The true loneliness of the long distance runner is a case in point, and a constructive factor. The great athletes of today have transcended their predecessors by achieving an inward mental isolation in which they confront only themselves, conquering their own weakness, reducing their rivals to irrelevance. That is how it is, on a lower plane, between me and the grouse as the moment of truth closes in. Their numbers are building up now in the heather out in front. Coveys have been edged forward by the drivers, a line of young men and girls converging on us from two miles out, and themselves still invisible. I can hear grouse-talk as I watch a merlin, that smallest and most graceful hawk, winnowing the air as it tracks some prey outside my butt, perhaps a fledgling pipit.

On the flank a white flag winks. A covey swing inwards, then straighten beyond a hummock where the next butt is. Two shots. Then three at the other end of the line. Another covey comes straight at me, seeming to accelerate hugely as the angular rate of change maximises overhead. Two grouse fall, their heather hues flashed with white as they tumble, turn over and are lost in their native element thirty yards apart. The air is sharp with cartridge smoke. Many more shots. When the drive is over the dogs go out, seeking the dead grouse birds lying hidden in it. To gundogs no other game is such a pleasure to retrieve as grouse. Whether because of the tightness of their feathers, or something especially wholesome in their smell, or the fact that to be out shooting again means return to duty after the summer lay-off, grouse are brought in with extra indications of triumph. The unuttered message is "Rejoice with me", not just "Here, take this".

The glory of August the Twelfth and after has passed into newspaper mythology. Personally I think 'glorious' an overstatement. To me it is just abundant pleasure. I feel about it rather as the dogs do. Everything is in its favour. Grouse shooting begets enjoyment, especially in good weather. Then the wind

and the sun invigorate, and sweethearts and wives are recognisable as such, their attractions unhidden by the storm-proof clothing needed on winter days at lowland game. There is a ready companionship, untrammelled by the anxieties, the tensions, those pregnant questions that hang in the air elsewhere ("Will the drive work out this time? What happened to the partridges on that beat? Will those fellows ever stop talking?"). If things do not go right on a grouse moor, there is plenty else to be cheerful about. Just being there, for instance.

Such, for me, is the grouse moor image. If, for some, the grouse moor image has an aura of proud looks and high stomachs, I can only say that I have never met it. Participation is a great equaliser, never more evident than high up in this sweet air. Presumably it elevates some, cuts others down to size, but there are no signs of which it is doing. Those who imagine otherwise are thinking of a social scene which, if it ever existed, had passed before my time. Old illusions die hard, being cherished by the media and, in this case, given an annual kiss of life each silly season.

One article of faith is that we are doing something that happens only in Scotland, an attenuated survival from a distant past still faintly extant in remote and undeveloped areas. Our impression is different, simply that we are doing something normal at this time of year along with many thousands elsewhere. We think the shooting is fairly good on these moors, but we know it is no better than in Yorkshire, often within sight of factory towns. We know also, though it may surprise some, that there are grouse moors in every Welsh county including Glamorgan of the steel and mines, in every Irish county, all over Scotland, in every English county north of the Trent, in Shropshire and Herefordshire also, and even a few grouse in Somerset. It is hardly a restricted pastime.

The day's shooting ends with the sun still high. When we come off the hill and down to the glens the grilse are running, the small salmon that come up the rivers after only one winter in the sea. Hours remain to try for one in the evening cool. By chance a full salmon, a true fush, may take the fly instead. And if neither obliges, a lighter rod may hook a sea-trout as day drains out of the sky.

We spend other days climbing high tops, or just wandering, or gathering fringe benefits; wild raspberries with their eager tang (the white ones are the more piquant), blaeberries on the hill, chanterelles from the woods. We gather golden moments too. In this seemingly empty land, something is always happening to mark the memory.

With a daughter I drift an upland loch for trout. The wind is lively and moves the boat too fast. We unship a sea-anchor to steady her. The rocky shore slides astern more slowly. It is a day of flying clouds and ever-moving duck; pochard come slanting in by the hundred, then teal, mallard and a few pintail. Generally at this time, with the eclipse close on them, duck stay in reed beds round home waters; occasionally, as now, mass wanderlust seizes them. I do not know the reason, nor the reason for much else, but it will be fun finding out as time goes by. They pitch into water the colour of a bay horse from the peat stain washed into it, but the spray they fling up is diamond bright. The wind has worked the water into scum lines, creaming it up like the head on a Guinness. Some trout hunt the scum lines for flies trapped in the edge of the foam, and we do not miss our opportunities. Dunkeld, black Pennell and claret-and-mallard do the trick, so are mentioned in dispatches.

With enough for a salad supper as well as for breakfast, we encounter the obverse side of Highland hospitality. An ancient ghillie presides over the ceremony of weighing the catch, recording our names, and admitting that the rowlocks have been returned. He accepts the normal handshake with a world-weary courtesy and comes down to earth when, shouldering our loads, we strike off across the heather, short-cutting to the ballast dump where the car is parked. He wouldna tra-vel yon road, he calls after us, on account of the groose birds. He predicts that the heid-kipper will smairten my airse wi' a cairtridge. Some airses, maybe, but I am willing to risk mine, the heid-kipper being no stranger.

Another day, another scene. We take a route across a broken

118

ridge into the next glen. There are more crags than heather on the way, interspersed with close-bitten turf and myriad rabbits. As always, the skyline recedes as we approach, then a sharp shower blots it out. Just short of the 2,000-ft contour we cross the spine and realise that we are losing height. A figure rears suddenly out of the mist, side-steps and vanishes into it again – a red stag, dripping from a roll in a peat pool, his antlers clotted with sphagnum moss – a sudden vision, there, then gone. I shall remember him in weeks to come.

Ten minutes later, with the outlook clearing, we see what had sent him hurrying uphill. There is better heather on this side and an English setter quests it ahead of a figure walking a little strangely because a peregrine sits on his angled, gauntleted arm. He is a falconer out for the grouse in the manner that anteceded gunpowder. From high above him we can keep him in view for an hour, so we find comfortable boulders and sit to eat our piece. We are still eating it when the setter points, flag high and rigid. Instantly the falcon is cast off, climbs in swinging circles above the small white dot of the dog, waiting-on for the game to be flushed. Then the setter moves forward, roading to the birds in the heather. What follows we can only guess; we are too far away to see. But the sequel is man and dog united, standing calmly together, so presumably the falcon, too small to be seen so far away, is back with them. If so a grouse, broken-backed by the force of the falcon's stoop, and sent hurtling earthwards, will have been safely gathered. That is Nature's way.

This is a daylong walk, and before the car reaches the rendez-vous to lift us home we are well and truly into midge time. When the sun's rays slant, the midge is the curse of Scotland. Perhaps it is midges that drive Scotsmen to drink, having impelled their forefathers to invent whisky to make life tolerable in their af-flicted land, and caused later generations to emigrate in such numbers that Scottish surnames proliferate round the world. Were I to compose a malediction, or pronounce an anathema, either would be against the Scottish midge which has caused so many good men to leave home, and others to start hitting the bottle promptly at six p.m. We have no bottles to hit.

Instead we have time to endure. Scottish midges are soft, silent, amorphous, not even readily visible, but certainly exceedingly tangible, with a capacity for torment unsurpassed elsewhere. They emerge from the heather in millions and gather in clouds round any warm-blooded life form, me for instance. They invade my eyes, tickle my ears, crawl under my scarf, down my neck, and up my sleeves. If I speak, I breathe them in, and start coughing. If I perspire they stick to my skin, kicking weedily. When they reach any skin not toughened by exposure to weather, they sting and set up an equally ineffective irritation which annoys but does not damage. Time was when I tried to repel them with pipe smoke. It did no good, even when I puffed so hard that bystanders thought I was trying to hide in a smoke screen. Others meet the menace in their own way. The feminine element in the party squirm prettily in silence. Their escorts slap themselves angrily, as if even a counter-masochism is better than no action at all. We have arrived nearly an hour before pick-up time. But where else could we have killed time free from this ubiquitous irritant? To pass the time I calculate how far we would need to go in reaching a midge-free zone. Caithness in the far North, Clackmannan to the South, respectively one hundred and two hundred and fifty miles away, seem the nearest.

A bunch of stots slither down the braeside and stand in the middle of the unfenced road, swinging their tails contentedly. For the first time I realise that the hairiness of Highland cattle is not for weather protection, but to keep the midges off. The beasts peer at us in our midge-infested purgatory from behind screens of overhanging eyebrow and forelock, licking their own noses and at peace with the world. The white-faced blacks, products of Hereford bulls on Friesian cows and much favoured by beef farms up here, have no such protection. They suffer greatly from midge-molestation of the eyes.

At last, as welcome as the trumpets of a relieving army, comes the sound of an approaching car. In these parts one can safely assume that the car expected is the only one there will be. We are not disappointed. It arrives dead on time.

"Where the devil have you been," we demand in midge-motivated petulance, wrenching open doors, flinging ourselves inside like the crew leaping aboard a fire engine, dropping knap-sacks on each other, and opening all the windows.

"Now drive, fast," is the urgent, unanimous order, and the swirling air drawn in and sucked out leaves us midge-free at last.

It has to happen some time. A tap on the barometer after dinner sends the mercury nearly out of sight. Next morning steel grey rain sweeps in under a steel grey sky, lashing the windows and rendering heroic he who braves it to exercise the dogs – an undertaking for which the dogs themselves have no enthusiasm whatever. Wet as it is, this is no ill wind. Letters are written that otherwise never would be, more drams than usual go the way of all their kind, records are played which would have gone unheard. We build up pressures of energy and frustration, ex-pending them at nightfall by driving storm-swept roads to a barn dance ten miles off. Of that kaleidoscopic evening few recol-lections remain save lusty men and personable women, endless noise in which figures whirled to rousing choruses, culminating in a pressing need for sleep.

Concentrations of humanity are not compulsive viewing for me, but one of those I do not miss is the Games. There is a Games within reach of every Highland burg, a distribution of about one per glen. At a distance these occasions project a sense of grandeur, even pomp and circumstance, and the presence of the mighty is assumed. But protocol is more imagined than ac-tual. Admittedly, it is a poor sort of Games which does not attract at least an earl, better still a duke, to give a pinnacle to the infrastructure of lairds, but what creates the atmosphere is the fact that everybody turns up, no less, and at no assemblies is mankind more equal. In their own parts, the spirit of the clans is still all-powerful and when Gordon meets Gordon or Ross accosts Ross (and so ad infinitum), whether magnate or loon, the confrontations are between equals. It is a matter of blood, as simple as that. Blood, which looms so large in Scottish history, is part of Scottish thinking too.

The kilt being much worn, tartan tells its story. To expert interpreters, the genetic mix of the ringside crowds is an open

book. Non-expert, I am concerned with more evident character-
istics. There is indeed a grandeur, but it is a private grandeur to
which we from afar are not admitted. We are welcome to watch,
to listen, at times to contribute, but we cannot be part of this
tight-knit occasion. We are frae doon sooth, and there is no
crossing that great gulf. My role is once again to go observing
matters, and no more.

The pipes skirl on. Well tuned-in judges assess the performance in terms of drone and chanter, and make the most presti-
gious awards in the Games. But the sound goes far beyond them,
permeating the whole concourse, lifting the crowds into a higher
consciousness of who and what they are. The pipes are a voice
of the nation – not mine but theirs, and a symbol of the differ-
ences. They may thrill others, in the way of all things rich and
strange, but they cannot move us and bind us as they move and
bind the Scots. Still from far off I watch the grace and gallantry
of the sword dancing, hear the grunts of weight-lifters, see the
swaying tree boles turning over at the last gasp of the strong
men at their butts. If I wait around until the participants join
the crowd, the oneness of mankind declares itself again. The
pipers, their wild music silenced, can use the same four-letter
words as other men; lissom lassies, down from the platform and
away now from their crossed blades, perspire behind their lace
jabots as all mortals do; and the brothy physiques of the caber-
tossers are centred round their brewer's muscles. Tip the bottle,
tell the tattle, get together, find the lady, today's the day; the
August sun will soon be setting, winter lasts a long time.

The morning after a Games is generally tailored for quiet re-
flection. It is likely to be a Sunday. Though the purists say that
Sabbath in Scotland is not what it was, any deterioration is
relative. The roads are thick with cars; not only the cars of
tourists, but of locals too, heading for beaches, sports meetings,
beauty spots, the Whisky Trail; all of which would have been
categorised by past elders as symptoms of perdition. Off the
roads, life is as it was. The hills and fields are silent. The only
energy expenditure is that of beef herds cudding. Homesteads
are quiet. All men's souls are their own, and most are also God's.

The seventh day is the Lord's day, and on it men do no manner of work nor any other thing which may be defined as an activity. Parallel with dimensions of the fourth Commandment, the Deity, the spirit and the conscience, the result is total peace. Because of their truth, some lines written by Charles Hilton Brown grafted themselves on to my mind long ago.

> Macpherson's gazing at the sheep,
> His lady for the armchair heading,
> The collie's out, the cat's asleep,
> The men are daunderin' roon' the steading.
>
> And I lie out among the heather
> And drink the soft consoling airs;
> A fine day after filthy weather...
> There's nothing to be done? Who cares?

The time comes to head South, down the long road up which we came. At half-way, the quietness of evening again enfolds the Border farm, the chuckling burn threads through the silence. Strolling before darkness falls, thinking of nothing in particular, the mind is blank enough for memories to be drawn into it by force of vacuum. They are all of peace and distance, of the far country now nearly all behind us, Scotland being a hard place to leave. More pictures in the mind. A pink-washed sheiling beside a sea-loch; the pipes heard out of doors and a long way off; that music uppermost in the Scottish heart, the lament; the stamping and the rhythms at the ceilidh; the haunting view where the sea stretches out to the ultimate North; the fiery sky where the sun sets beyond the Hebrides, a bar of gold across the Minch in its wake; the nostalgia, the faith and the magnetism; voices singing, "Will ye no' come back again?"

Yes.

AFTER another day of travel, shadows are falling round the gates of home. From the motorway we drove through a different world. Instead of far Scottish views, always a range of mountains looming and another beyond that, Wessex is close-knit; instead of the sparseness of granite and heather, fields are tight with ungathered harvest. The evening mist adds a sleepiness, the indistinctness of a dream, to things long familiar; to thatched white cottages drowsing knee-deep in corn, low-pitched roofs seeming lower than ever because the ground line has been raised to the height of the standing crop. Roads are wet and the air sweet from a recent shower, evidently not the only one. The farmers have been waiting their chance, and not getting it. Only a few fields scattered along the route have been cleared to stubble, doubtless winter-sown barley. The rest still wait.

Indoors, somebody switches on the news. For the past weeks it has not seemed to matter. It does not seem to matter now; tuning-in the mind to pseudo-urgencies takes time; but at least the forecast is good. And in fact the next day's sun rises free of cloud, quickly burning off the dew. The sound-effects of our first morning at home contrast with weeks of Highland silence and recall the talk of bygone years.

In days now gone we used to talk of harvest hum. Those were days when horses powered the job, when senior workmen drove the reapers, the strongest men pitched the sheaves, and every other available pair of hands wielded prong and rake – days which I can just remember among memory's own first harvests. But harvest hum did not mean what it sounds. The words were west-of-Severn mispronunciation of harvest home. We could not know their prophetic significance. For now, as the mist lifts off and leaves the grain full, red and hard so that fears of drying costs recede, the harvest literally begins to hum on all sides. Over all England, as combine after combine starts up and adds its voice to that of the next, a great sound-wave spreads nation-wide. The climax of the productive year gains pace until the harvest hum grows into the harvest roar. Behind the muffled-thunder of the combines' engines the tractors join in, clattering out to tow grain wagons into which, driven alongside, the moving combines blow their cargo. Once set moving, modern harvesting does not pause.

In the days of which I had been thinking, perpetual motion was not possible. But synchronisation was just as important, and more complex. There were more people to synchronise. There was also a set procedure, a due sequence in which the work was approached, and a certainty that if the sequence was not fulfilled lips would be pursed, heads would wag, and a general air of no-good-will-come-of-this would supervene. The age of simplification had not then dawned. The modern combine does more than merely convert cutting and threshing into one operation. Because its cutters are positioned forward it can be driven straight into a crop and from the very first drills will instantly begin to cut, pick up and thresh, holding back the grain and spewing out the empty straw like some great mastodon taking the cream of all in its path. But the reaping machines which preceded combines were pulled by horse or tractor, their cutter bars mounted at right angles under the wheeling feeder arms. They could not cut and gather the crop directly ahead of them because it would have been trampled or flattened by the horse or tractor. So a first swath round the field had to be taken out by scythe, and these first sheaves were hand-bound.

It was a process stiff with tradition, in which seniority counted heavily. Throughout my life the scythe, long the harvester's basic tool, has been receding into obsolescence. But in my family it was a tradition that every boy should learn to use one; he could not become a man unless he did, and I am thankful to those stern ancestors who saw that I was taught. If they can look down from whatever Valhalla their spirits now inhabit (and I would not put it past them) they must think my occasional present performances lamentable; I can hear them saying, "Very sloppy!" But at least I can do it, which in these days makes me almost unique in the village. So I might have been included in the select minority who in those days could have joined in opening out a field. We would have entered it with the blessing, variously expressed, of the lord of the harvest.

This title generally went to the oldest old gaffer on the farm, probably one who had long since received the local equivalent of the Chiltern Hundreds. His implied function of chief executive was much more apparent than real; he was, in fact, a figurehead. But the institution had its values in an age when farming was labour-intensive and the human factor less sophisticated than it has now become. To be lords of the harvest was a way of giving jobs to die-hards long past work but not admitting it, and who would otherwise have become well-intentioned obstructionists. Safe on their pedestals, whence to interfere would be beneath their dignity, at least they took the blame if weather failed.

Whoever worked through those harvest days was a fit man as well as an honest one. Though demands on strength and stamina are different now, the land will always be a hard taskmaster. What the stresses were then, memory makes me well aware; in retrospect my muscles have not ceased their seasonal aching yet. Pitching up sheaves by prong on to the wagons was probably the greatest energy spender. It was all overarm work, shoulder height or above, and very much above when the load grew to ten feet high. The first of life's lessons in farm work is the difference between overarm and underarm, the second being the skill with which experienced operators can convert one into the other or, if they cannot, ensure that somebody else does it. An even greater back-breaker, because of attitude, was (and in crofting Scotland continues to be) stooking up. This means gathering the sheaves and building them six at a time into stooks, ears uppermost so that wind and sun can dry them before stacking. The work develops an unholy rhythm of bending and lifting sheaves, then ramming them hard into the ground so that their stalks interlace with the standing stubble. Just putting them there is not enough; they must be forced hard downwards or they will not stand – and woe betide the binder who puts the ties too low.

Days later the ambling harvest wagon would come round, the horses walking the lines with the skill of experience, guided only by gruff "Haw" and "Gee". With two men on top and two on foot, all with prongs, the sheaves were pitched and loaded. Then came the definitive moment of "leading", the click of the tongue which made the horses lean into their collars, the muscles of

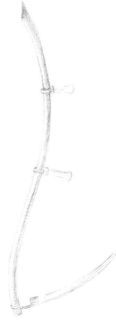

their quarters bulging, and a mighty, co-ordinated heave set the loaded wagon moving homewards, dipping and rolling across the shaven field. In more than one sense wagons were the ships of the land. Hence the skill of building their cargoes on their open decks, piled high because the bigger the load the fewer the journeys and the quicker and cheaper the job. Every yard of every trip had to be foreseen and calculated; every camber in the lanes, every slope in the lie of the land, the tightness of every turn, the clearance under every overhanging branch. One thing was just about as easy as falling off a log, and that was sending home a wagon with a load that would overturn. To avoid it, the kind of sense was needed that is not learned at universities.

Each separate journey was the culmination of months of toil, weather, and faith. The farmer's money was coming home. It had been laid out a year before, just after the previous harvest. In the meantime flood, storm and frost had threatened it, sun and rain had nourished it; and with God's help more came back than went out. On that margin depended the fortunes of the farm and of everybody on it. It was not seed corn alone that was turning-in its yield. Muck, luck, judgment and hard work played their part as well. When the wagons came safely in, everybody knew it, and in due course were thankful.

But before that, there was more to be done. In the farmyard every wagon load had to be pitched again, built into a stack that would be rain-proof, wind-proof, vermin-proof. There it would stay until Winter, when the steam-engine hissed and puffed along the lanes, towing the threshing machine and all its gear. Then the stacks so laboriously built would be opened, the prongs would go in again, and for as many days as it took, the elevator hoisted sheaves in endless succession, grain was knocked out in the drum and piped down to waiting sacks, and mountains of golden straw grew taller. On clumping feet, a ceaseless file of men humped sacks up the outside stairway to the granary over the stables. At the door, as much a key figure as the lord of the harvest and more useful, a dour little Hunt terrier stood to intercept any rat that might try to sneak in too.

If the threshing machine came in school holidays, my role was at the foot of the elevator, armed with a sharp knife, slashing the twine that bound each sheaf. A modern Safety Officer would have vertigo at the mere idea, but it was good to be part of the communal effort, and warm there too in the lee of the pulsating steam engine, with its great fly-wheel, driving-belt, and glowing fire-box, source of all power and progress. The chill wind blew all round the scene, enveloping it in showers of chaff so that men went coughing in the yellow dust. When halt was called for mid-morning "allowance", for dinner or tea, or at day's end, the effects were apparent. No matter who had done what, from the jolly oil-streaked engineer down to the humble twine-cutter, all of us had yellow arms and faces; when we shook ourselves or did busman's fling (as we had to do before the feasting followed) the dust flew out in clouds. Only when all the grain was in the granary was harvest truly home, and the steam-engine free to chuff along more lanes to the next farm, belching steam and crushing flint chippings to powder beneath its iron wheels. Some people talked of the harvest dragon, but we called him Puffing Billy.

Now it can all happen in a day if all goes right.

I do not want the days of memory back, even though I believe that the sum of human happiness was greater when more men and fewer machines produced our daily bread. The world changes; we live as things are, not as they were; clocks tick on, calendars go and others come. Now, after decades as a spectator of the farming scene, I see three men do in two weeks what twenty would have needed a month to achieve in those past years. The combine now is the ship of the land, a great lumbering tanker that moves no faster than the horses did, but does four jobs simultaneously as it goes.

No skills and effort are needed with the prong now. All is untouched by hand. Today a virgin field is thick with richness, the crop's ears bowed by the grain's own weight and hot in the sunshine, a cool residual moisture round its roots. Enter the combine, clanking and jerking in. The crops sighs as it collapses and is clawed-in to the threshing chamber. Straw churns out in the combine's wake. The grain is tanked up internally until a pay-load is ready. Then a tractor ranges alongside, holds its pace and a blower ejects corn in a golden cascade, self-winnowed by the breeze as it falls into the trailer. Within minutes the load is back at the farm, piped by pressure, suction or augur into silos, and the tractor returns to refill. Perhaps another tractor tows a baler into the field, shaping the straw windrows into rectangles to be picked up by a buckrake; perhaps not; and if not, smoke will darken the sky. Modern harvest is quick. It is efficient. But it is not easy. No work well done is ever that. If I did not know that much already, I know it when I see it happen.

The combine makes its vibrating crawl along a headland, grazing-off its first bellyful of the day, heading directly towards me. In the cool of the morning I can feel its heat twenty-five yards away. High up in his cockpit, my neighbour is dwarfed by the mass of metal around and under him. He has no eye for me, and seems depersonalised in consequence. All his mind, all his heart, so presumably all his soul also, are in what he is doing; conning the course of a great vehicle not easy to steer, seeing his way, calculating the line of the turn he must soon make, checking all systems, watching his dials. His ear-defenders symbolise his isolation from the world in which I stand. His expression is wrapt, intent, abstracted yet concentrated, the face of a saint at prayer or, not dissimilar, of a craftsman at his work, expressing total commitment.

In and out with grain trailer and baler, his sons' tractors converge on the moving combine like destroyers round a battleship. There will be no straw-burning here, but doubtless plenty elsewhere. I am relieved, but not greatly so. It is a practice which over-excites good-hearted people – more of them living in towns than in the country. The closer one lives to the land, the more one knows about it, and I do not share all their concern. Straw-burning causes heart-burning, but if properly done, I do not think it damages much wild life. It certainly harms some, but so does ploughing. If straw-burning is overdone, or improperly done, it is human interests which chiefly suffer. I feel sorry for the field voles, which I believe do suffer whether straw-burning is done properly or not. But their fate is no worse than that on a vastly greater scale of the rats and mice which local authorities exterminate in mass, and would fail their duty if they did not. No voices are raised in their defence by those so voluble on other issues. Rats and mice have feelings too, but nobody, not even protesters at straw-burning, seems to pity them. The worst thing about straw-burning is that it is obvious, even spectacular. It looks bad, so it must be bad, so townsfolk come to think. Less so to me, seeing it happen and after.

I have been watching eighteen acres where wheat was harvested. After combining, the straw lay in windrows for a week. Partridges called at dusk as they had done before the crop was cut. A hare lobbed off in the evenings from a form presumably shaded under the straw from the day-long glare. I would be surprised if a brood or two of late pheasants did not come and go. Scattered across the field, many families of voles and long-tailed field mice, well dug in, would have survived the passing of the combine above their heads. Thrushes hopped and foraged on the ground newly cleared between the windrows; so did a few blackbirds, yellowhammers and pipits. Then the straw was burned.

As the smoke clouds rolled downwind, the red line of flame at their base, anything winged had every chance to move out. No doubt it was taken; birds have no Casabianca complex; fire means death, and all who can take flight do so. I did not see the hare escape, though evidently she did. If a flightless pheasant brood was caught mid-field, they would have been doomed by holocaust, but to be still in the chick stage as late in the year as this would be unusual, and their life expectation not good. The lengthening nights, oncoming storms and autumn frosts, all soon to come, raise the odds against them. Some of the mice and voles might have been burned alive, but probably only few; rather more would have been asphyxiated underground, losing the fight for breath and choking (the fate which anti-hunting organisations recommend for foxes) as the flames swept overhead.

It was evening; and now it is morning on the next day, and I continue to watch where the burn-off happened. True, indeed, that the field may look like a desert to others, but not to me, and not to birds. The land is singed, not charred. The news-distribution systems of wild life work their usual miracle. The coast is twenty miles away, but within two hours of sunrise three hundred gulls move in. So do the eighty rooks from the village colony, much reduced now by the absence of elms. A liberal scattering of lapwings also arrive, a blue-grey patch of feeding woodpigeons, assorted starlings and jackdaws. The thrushes, blackbirds and pipits cannot be seen. They may have been out-numbered to the point of invisibility by the newcomers, or the burning destroyed their soft-bodies insect and invertebrate food species, so they have gone elsewhere.

What do all the others find, to attract so many of them? Anybody's guess is as good as mine. Mouse flambé may well be a delicacy for seagulls and rooks and some others; but, even in infestation numbers, the supply could not keep so many probing beaks busy for so long. Perhaps charred weed seeds and grain are as much appreciated by some birds as roasted peanuts are by us. The certainty is that those eighteen acres are regarded as more of a land of plenty after they have been burned than they were before.

At last light I walk across them with my dogs. Late as it is, we still put up feeding woodpigeons. From out of nothing (except, of course, her now unshaded form) the hare appears and, ears high, is off on her nightly business. As we head home partridges call to my receding back from somewhere out in the empty expanse. What seems to motorists on the distant road an

act of total destruction to the natural scene, has left most of the residents carrying on as usual. Fire comes, fire goes, life continues. For them straw-burning is just another thunderstorm, or just another blizzard with death by fire instead of drowning or freezing – so long, of course, as it does not get out of hand. For weeks yet there will be smudges in the sky as varying winds give farmers new chances to burn fields along safe lines.

MEANWHILE, colours change. The land turns golden as the year ripens. Americans talk of their Fall with an almost holy zeal. I have seen it once. Our version cannot excel it for intensity, especially the key-note red of maples. But in its total colour our Autumn is at least the Fall's equal; in my eyes it's superior, being bred into my blood, which is warmed by the sight of it.

Chlorophyll is sinking back into the earth, and with it the green is drained from the countryside. Hedgerow fruits give richer colours to glow between the ochre and umber of shorn fields, new tilth and turning woodlands. Blackberries, elderberries, sloes, crabs, hips and haws, bullace and many more hang gleaming in the cooler sunshine which now floods the land. In another month oak leaves will be yellow, russet beech leaves fly in showers, and ash trees drop their foliage each in a single night, but more time must pass first. Autumn cannot be hurried. Having declared its dividends both farmed and wild, the countryside now pauses to show off its products in its own harvest festival.

Still brighter colours come and go. The long-lived, pollen-rich late flowers have feasts for butterflies. Under the afternoon sun, a buddleia bush is almost hidden by heraldic-patterned wings all opened and vectoring to soak in the source of life. Red admirals, scarlet on black; gorgeous peacocks; painted ladies; fritilliaries, of dashing flight; tortoiseshells, large and small; the ragged-winged but graceful commas all gather, dancing in the air, settling, revelling, unrolling their long tongues for the bliss in the florets, forcing an overflow meeting on some nearby Michaelmas daisies.

In the background three cables cross the stableyard – power supply, telephone and an internal intercom line from the house. Swallows are perching on them. Silhouetted against the sky, they look like the notes on a musical score. They are forming up for their migration flight back to Africa. I wonder what they will find to perch on, there in the drought-stricken semi-desert south of the Sahara. Fewer convenient, tight, parallel cables for sure. Instead, perhaps steep-sided sandstone bluffs, baked within an hour of each equatorial dawn; perhaps twigs in the speckled shadow of savannah trees. I do not envy them their journey to the wider world. In my experience it consists largely of discomforts.

In the small world of the village, we respond with the rest of Nature to the surge and ebb of life. Summer warmth lingers and there is plenty all around, but each day is shorter than the one before. This diminuendo gears up all forms of life, animate or otherwise, to take heed for the future. Barren months of Winter, the starvation time, cast their fears ahead; the wherewithal to meet them is available now. So every living thing increases its substance by feasting – as a precaution, not a celebration. There is only one place for storage, and that is under the skin, or its equivalent.

The shortening days are the time when plants which will stand the Winter grow ever faster as they build up their reserves. Cabbages heart up, turnips swell, apples pack the resources of sap and sunshine round their pips, concentrating vigour to nourish the seedlings when they germinate. Birds live in luxury on fallen weed seeds, berries, and the newly-multiplied invertebrate life of top-soil; they scratch, they seek; they peck and gain weight; their new plumage blooms with well-being. Every animal from mouse to bullock grows round and bonny; the sight of a rib is a thing of the past, or of the future. For the present, all is well covered in the high gloss of good living.

These weeks of fulfilment bring upsurges of activity on the human level, too. The parson organises Harvest Festival, largely for parishioners otherwise in church only for weddings and funerals. Except for a battle, there is nothing like harvest to produce a resurgence of religion. In face of these simplicities we know Whom to thank and in Whom we trust. In more worldly moments, men tell their wives to lay on harvest suppers, at which best suits are worn by tanned, muscular men who tuck in, drink deep, and laugh anew at jokes they have been hearing for years. Other ladies, less close to the land, organise the handicraft show. Needlework, cakes, jam, flowers, pictures, perfumes, home-made wines and other marvels are all displayed there for mutual admiration, and to speed the passing year. We can still hope for one more Saturday on which summer hats may grace the grand occasion. Such finery then hibernates through the rain-swept months to come.

One nightfall breaks the pattern. Westward, the sky is stacked with clouds. The wind, which has built them into towers of cumulo-nimbus, gusts over us, rattling windows and reviving long-forgotten draughts. A working party is organised to bring under cover the garden furniture on which we sun-bathed. Thus the gale begins, the equinoctial gale which annually gives fair warning that the supremacy of day over night is ended, and that henceforth the balance will tilt the other way. After dark it gathers strength. Towards morning heavy rain, flung against the panes, tells me that this is the real thing, and that three rough days lie ahead. Morning comes in gun-metal grey, the wind blows more strongly still, now with a settled pressure.

The orchard presents an ominous sight. With full loads of fruit, apple branches rise and fall like a swelling sea, their precious burden undulating as if the whole crop is floating in stormy waters. I have known strong men, their money at stake, utter coarse words at such a sight, and have myself done likewise in past years. But not now. Our apples are well behaved. Though

135

they will part from the tree at a hand's turn, wind does not dislodge them. They ride out any storm until the second week of October; after which they store at their best, and keep until after Easter.

Two more desk-weather days, two more loud and windy nights, and the equinox has made its point. Calm returns, that steady, luminous, golden age that in a good year spans late September, all October and, if humanity is especially lucky, spills into November and permits the deserving householder to harvest dry carrots on Guy Fawkes' day. Meanwhile the agenda is full.

The weather steadies after the gale. Life of all kinds resumes its measured programmes. Days start with a cool promise and, with parity between darkness and light, the dawn is again part of my day. There is a stillness now, the stillness of equipoise. Morning mists linger, holding back the autumn fragrances for connoisseurs to savour. As always, the best of the day is in the hours before breakfast.

One special sunrise dazzles across a stubble field, which shines as if it were a lake. Gossamer spiders have arrived, riding on the night airs, each navigating his thread like Thames watermen drifting lighters upstream. Now the webs have been spun and anchored on the stubble spears, joining up to form an uninterrupted cover. At a rough estimate of a four-inch square per web I reckon an overnight input of 396,900 spiders on one acre. It seems a great many airborne spiders to have travelled together so suddenly. I wonder where they started, how they took off, and how they managed to land in such close order. When we look at the small things around us, ordinary features of Creation, one thing is obvious. We do not know it all, not yet.

Up the slanting track and on to downs, the feeling of Autumn is in the air, and at my feet the trumpet flowers of bindweed, purple vetch, late cornflower. Cock pheasants explore at hedge-foot, the sunshine striking lights from the copper and green of their new feathers. The sharp breathing and three-beat rhythm of cantering racehorses sends a partridge covey flying.

Days later, when next I see the like of them, ancient Britain stretches as far as I can see. We are out for the season's first walk-up where partridges skim on convex wings across the great emptiness devoted to tanks and missiles. The weather forecasters call it central southern England, and much of it is Salisbury Plain, a deceptively peaceful-sounding designation. Periodically by day or night the plateau flashes and shudders to gunfire, shell burst, explosions, and the vibration of great engines of destruction passing by. Then quiet follows and the landscape is as it has been since the glaciers melted and plants returned. The morning wind whispers through the sparse wild grasses, the bennets and the rushes just as it whispered in the ears of the unknown men who for unknown reasons created the immense geometry of Avebury, or brought vast stones from Wales to build into other temples to the sun. The wide hills are as dotted with wind-racked thorn bushes as they always were, bushes that gave cover to runaways and highwaymen, guerrillas and invaders, the small fry of our history.

Driving to the meeting place I pass Stonehenge, the unanswered question. Huge and enigmatic, the great structure outlasts another year, another century, possibly another civilisation. Did the impulses which drove men to this mighty work die with them? Or did it constitute forgotten truth, which in some submerged way lives on? I wonder what other men in other days have thought as they set eyes on these great stones – the Roman armies, for instance, as they marched by. In their imperial service they must have seen strange sights, as we did in ours. Perhaps they grew accustomed to the mysteries of subject peoples, and just ignored them. Or perhaps they saw more than is left to us.

Their first impression was two thousand years nearer to the time when Salisbury Plain was not our island's empty quarter but its metropolis, with a population large enough to fill amphitheatres as big as Wembley Stadium, a people so confident of their own significance that their graves remain on every side. Generally in sevens, sometimes in threes or fives, their collapsed tombs which we call barrows are always beside tracks which once were major routes. The biggest of all barrows are at crossroads. Human nature being what it is, no doubt it mattered as

137

much then as now to live at a good address; but to be buried beside a fashionable thoroughfare, where passers-by could see the monument for generations afterwards, mattered even more. Individuality outlasted death. It was not quite eternal life, but a step towards that human aspiration.

We climb one of the barrows to scan the country, to gauge the wind, to fix bearings for our advance. There are quiet clicks as guns are loaded and breeches closed. The bygone bigwigs who sleep beneath our feet will surely forgive us; we mean no disrespect. There is a haze, perhaps of coming thunder, and a sun-shimmer over the miles ahead, where the land is growing paler as the year grows older. The view sinks into dead ground and rises beyond; the breeze comes head-on; the first Autumn lark song spills out of the sky; from some half-bare ground chewed up by heavy vehicles into semi-desert, an unseen stone curlew smacks his bill like the clapper-board in a film studio.

We dozen men are ready to go a dozen miles in expectation of very little. The wild partridges of Wessex, bred across generations for survival in this setting, know well how to take care of themselves. Our problem is not of marksmanship, but of field-craft in putting them over the guns; or in some other way bringing the guns within range.

That task is really one for pointers or setters, the bird-locating dogs which in their disciplined gallop taste the wind across a quarter-mile front, giving fifty yards warning of the coveys lying ahead, and enabling shooters to move into position before the birds rise. But this classic skill is rare now in southern England. The dogs that have it, and the men and women who can work them, are mainly in grouse country further north. My spaniels, being close range operators, are no substitute. Nevertheless they are with me. They will have their moments, mainly as retrievers after the day's few shots are fired. But the real reasons for their presence are the mental and physical exercise. To clear their wind, to convert flesh to muscle, to test concentration, to find their noses, to continue the revival of game-sense which began on the Scottish moors, are all necessary preliminaries to the shooting days ahead.

Lined out across the shadeless Plain, we kick back the miles under a strengthening sun. A covey bursts into the air with a whirr of wings, too far out to be shot. We halt, watch them pitch down half a mile on, and memorise where. In due course we flush them again and they fly further; still we move on to lift them yet again. Next time they feel themselves so far from home that instead of flying on they turn back over our heads. The gunshots sound flatly in the vast, echoless space. Some birds fall, to lie small and invisible in dead rough grass faded as brown as they are. Out goes a spaniel, all quivering eagerness and flashing tail. As satisfying as a clean-killing shot is the sight of a gundog which knows its work. Questing the ground upwind, missing no yard of it, checking each tussock, it signals scent. There follows a brisk rummage around until the partridge is found tucked under overhanging fogg and brought to hand.

By lunchtime a few more coveys have broken back, but we dozen are still a party of small expectations. However we have become philosophical also. Contented by effort and exercise, richer for the touch of the sun, the free air and the wide view, we nevertheless feel one lack. Each of us looks forward to the first frost, that astringent moment after which we live hard until another Spring. When it comes, within a week, it is only fore-warning. The first frost has no venom. It is typical of October, that sane, stable, mellow interlude when the air is as golden and as refreshing as the wine which the month produces.

Now all our counties lie at ease, from Cape Wrath to the Channel shore. The fields are peaceful, their duty done. The woods still hold their leaves. Mornings sparkle and the noons are still. Well may the bees think now that warm days will never cease, days that pass slowly in the short golden age which is Autumn.

When else can Autumn be? We think and talk much about this elusive season, yet its share of the calendar is minimal. September is late Summer, most of the time. November is Winter more often than not. Only October, golden October, is neither one nor the other but genuine, incontestable Autumn. It is a time of quickening activity, but of quietness too, as if the weather were music and playing a nocturne to the declining year.

Cats are sunbathing when I walk the village street, conscious of their luck before the coming storms. So are the senior dogs, and some of the senior citizens. Old ladies snip chrysanthemums in front gardens, geraniums are being removed from porches to living rooms, an infallible first sign of Winter's approach. These small things in this sublime and reliable month, remind me of life's greater stabilities.

NEVER go back. That advice is freely given when we talk of times gone. Things remembered may seem shrunk, or aged, or turned to dust and ashes on reacquaintance, so the pessimists warn against. But I am no pessimist and October brings a chance to revisit my beginning.

It was easy to bend a journey round the Shropshire village which I knew before I had seen a town, still less a city. Life unfolded there. Every happening was new and so, however trivial, each was a major event to me. Like chickens hatching, for example. My first exercise in creation was to chip away the eggshells, taken at the critical moment from under the broody, help the quivering newcomers free, and put them to dry on the hearth of the old Jacobean kitchen, snug in a worn-out hunting hat. Now that I have seen more men die than chickens hatch, and a different world supplant the one I knew, a pilgrimage would prove to me that I really lived those days and have not been dreaming since.

Along the lanes that Puffing Billy took, sprays from the hedges tap the windows of the car. As things have been, they remain. It was the same when we went by dog-cart. In the curiosity of childhood I would reach out sideways and sideways again to grab at leaves on either side, learning life's first lesson in botany – what is thorned and what is not. The Autumn sunshine long ago left for ever in my senses the unforgettable smell of warm leather. It blew from seats and reins and harness, blending with air vitalised by the warm clean pony trotting between the shafts and kicking up dust which sired a thirst for ginger beer. That would be slaked when, escorted by looping greenfinches, we came to the village street. Behold, there are greenfinches now.

Symbolic outriders of a friendly power, they welcome the return of a native as they fly ahead of the car which moves ever slower while I seek the first recognition from old times. The dipping lane winds down between high banks. I find myself looking left. A faintly villainous cottage used to be the first building. It still is, and as villainous, still the hereditary tenement of a

village bad lot a generation later. The suspense tightens. Another bend will expose the house which once was ours. Time now to prepare for change and decay or, perhaps even less acceptable, the new glory that comes from a rich man's whim. Run-down or tarted up, I brace myself for shock and receive instead a reassurance so total that I stop the car and sit and gaze.

Half-timbered, black and white, chequered by pargetting, it stands the same as ever, a homecoming as unsurprising and as total as if my absence had been a mere term away at school. Knowing where to look, I note the door of the back lobby, an entrance sacred to those returning weather-beaten and mud-spattered from hunting, shooting, or just plain farming. The door is swinging in the wind. It always did. Epochs of history have come and gone, and still its latch fails to hold. How many have failed and been replaced meanwhile? At a crawl, the car draws past the frontage. Beyond the low wall hollyhocks are bending with old age. There were always hollyhocks, beside damp stone steps leading to an abandoned well. In Spring and Summer there were always wallflowers, sweet williams, columbines, and phlox. So there will be again.

Still slowly, the car moves on. On the left, inside the church-yard gate, a dark column tops a mound. My forebears lie in the vault beneath. The dead of Salisbury Plain were not alone in reminding their successors of their passing presence here. The village street winds rightward. The dog-cart used to stand outside the grocer's, where the street is wider. The car can do the same.

In few villages can a return after four decades find every expectation fulfilled, as this one does. It is stone-built, the dark unweathering iron-bearing stone of Coalbrookdale and thereabouts. Its buildings are as near indestructible and immoveable as makes no odds. Before I open the shop door I know well what will happen when I do. The surrealism of return in time as well as place intensifies. The bell will ting when the door opens, I shall take two steps down, and the grocer will look up at me, watchful behind his bacon-slicing machine, half-right beyond the jars of sweets.

Is he also feeling, uncomfortably as we all are at such moments, that all this has happened before? We stare at each other, too intently for good manners it seems to me. But this grocer is only thirty-five, at most thirty-eight. There cannot be recognition. He was not born when last the bell went ting for me.

"By no means," he says. "No inconvenience at all." Nobody will be troubled however long I leave my car outside his shop. His speech reopens the lost world, north Midland rough but laced with the cadence of Wales. We seem again to be looking too long at each other, perhaps because time is standing still. It needs a major effort to set it moving again. I thank him, and leave.

There is no ribbon development here; no new buildings anywhere, so it seems, except wide-span stressed concrete barns and cattle courts on the farms which once were run by those in the vault. Strangely it is the transient, not the material objects, which confirm the long memories. Free air blows over the meadows, spiced with the scents of grass; from a gateway in a dip, as much poached as it used to be, the mud exhales the richness of the earth; a paddock where hunters stretched their legs, wearing rugs after being clipped of their winter coats, has hunters in it now; a dank tangle of elders and fading nettles is loud with the croak of moorhens; a brook, unseen but known to me, splashes in its stoney bed. The smells, the sounds, the sights – in that order the most evocative senses – recreate the world I knew when the close-up world mattered most.

One must start somewhere; and to where one starts, the heart goes back. Strangely, I feel no sense of isolation at being in this familiar place without the family now gathered under the dark column. Except for the grocer, I make only one human contact.

At the old house I am received by a lady in brisk middle age. Hearing my name she stares as if I had risen from the vault. "We thought you were all dead," she says, "dead, or emigrated." I explained that some of us survived, but in tail-female now. "It comes from in-breeding," she said. Too true.

It is tea-time. Will I join her? On second thoughts, would I prefer something stronger, some gin perhaps? Gin at four-thirty

143

is not my habit, but I accept. Here, within four walls, the past is pressing closer. Curving up from a fire-lit hall the staircase seems ready to echo its lost voices, the high spirits that made the house a place of noise and vigour. Remembering them, waiting for them, to be urbane is difficult.

Seeing my gaze focussed on a corner cupboard, she says, "My parents bought most of the furniture along with the house. It was the only way really, with everybody waiting for the invasion." It was one way of putting it. Those of us who were young did not in those days give much thought to seeing home again. Afterwards, in retrospect, now, the full truth dawns. Having seen much else – London, most of Britain, much of Europe, East of Suez, the New World, Arctic ice and equatorial forests – and having watched my share of history happen, the most firmly etched of all the memories are those of this old house, its small village, the surrounding fields and woods. We Saxons have our roots, and they go deep.

Day is nearly done when I take leave. The grocer has closed his shop. I open the car door and take a last look. Living room windows along the street are lit. Their homely comfort warms the coming evening. The open road beyond the village leads past a spinney. There the oak boles show silvery against the deepening shadows, the same oak boles that a small boy hurried past at this time of day because they looked like a line of ghosts. Only Shropshire oaks do that. Some combination of soil and weather, of humidity and lichen nourished by the winds from Wales, gives them their luminosity.

It is a long way to Wessex. Often have I told myself that miles are shorter going home. But where is home?

FOR the next few months home is where the wet road leads, wending over the hills, shining in the rain. As the hours of daylight shorten, home will receive me back from days in open country, where rough weather replaces the touch of the sun. After effort, wind and downpour home means warmth and rest. Home is where tea and toast are ready, lights shine, voices welcome me, fires glow, bath and soft clothes are waiting. Winter, the season for homecoming, is giving forewarnings now.

The first morning fog is one of them. It is not mere mist, the transient lifting of the night's condensed moisture from the land. It comes sharp as snuff to the nostrils. It is dense enough to throw back echoes, confusing ears as well as eyes. Even on familiar ground, men must watch their bearings, animals and birds lose their way.

Preceded by a rumble of squelching footsteps, a dozen bullocks go storming past as I cross their field. They have no eyes for me but stare ahead, vainly seeking some landmark now hidden. After the fog has swallowed them I hear them trampling round at a right angle to their previous direction, still mystified. Then my spaniel also loses contact. Unwisely, I whistle. Seconds later she flashes past, a blurred figure anxious and at full stretch; then is gone again. Dogs' hearing is more sensitive, more analytical than ours, but the sound of the whistle is reaching her from all angles, echoing off the drifting walls of fog, confusing her instead of guiding her. Realising this, I stand silent until she finds me by patient nosework and we move on, together again, to flight pigeons on upland clover. They are disorientated in a different way. For an hour they come in, singly along the same line directly overhead, and to get forty is not difficult. Nor is it exhilarating. But forty fewer greedy beaks are left to attack the kale in the next field, sown as emergency ration for the dead of the year.

How strange that evolution, which has familiarised all life with night and day, should leave creatures still mystified by fog. Horses can see in what to us is darkness. They seldom shy or jib when led past unfamiliar objects at night. But in fog they see ghosts. Unless given confidence by voice and hand and leg, their momentary fear escalates into panic. Better to be on foot this morning, when visibility is down to ten yards, admiring the cobwebs which lace the hedgerow, pearled with droplets.

On such a day as this my mind is back in Scotland. Stags are roaring there, far away in the Highland haar, closing the incomparable weeks of deerstalking. There, above all, is mercy in the act of killing for sport, and for such killing a real need, making a complete expression of the sportsman's code. The stag has no awareness that his death is near; if he becomes aware, he moves and thereby ceases to be in danger. When a stag falls it is to a bullet delivered with surgical precision from close range. The unwritten laws of stalking are that the firer of the rifle shall wait until the chosen beast is in an attitude which ensures not merely a hit but a clean kill.

For those who do it, a deer stalk is a long day of concentration, insulation, and endurance. Many miles fall behind, whole mountains go underfoot. The spy glass takes in the smallest details of miles-wide wind-hollowed vistas, topped by scree and broken by shadowed corries. Professional stalkers are skilled, fit men. They find the deer, grazing far away, choose a stag ready to be killed, and bring the "rifle" (he or she who shoots) into position to fire the shot. The approach across wild rough country must be lined between scent-bearing airstreams which, even at a range of miles, alert the deer to human approach. This is fieldcraft at its most testing, an art so fine that its attractions are as compelling for women as well as men.

A perfect stalking day involves one shot. When total effort has been expended on one chosen beast, total difficulties overcome and his execution fulfilled, there is no time for any more. That act represents a moment only in a day-long contest with Nature and the unwitting quarry. Success in this, the mountain magic, and the patience rather than the culmination, are the stuff of triumph. Some people, never having done it, cannot share the stalker's sense of achievement. It conflicts with their reverence for life, which I share. What I cannot do is to extend that reverence into a belief that to take life can never be morally right. This, in the present context, would at first increase the deer population *ad infinitum*, regardless of the facts that the space and food on which they live cannot be increased, and numbers expanded beyond resources mean starvation, degeneration and disease. Life has a logic, and a balance, in which death is the counterpoise. It applies to all species, including our own. Stalkers replace the wolf packs which in evolution operated that counterpoise.

At far distance, and in retrospect, I see the day unfolding. In the glens, men and women wake up in hotels and lodges with long days before them; days of long walking and of climbing, of fording rivers, crawling sodden-clad along burns, lying-up in peat hags, enduring storms, being scorched by the sudden sunshine of the high tops. Boots crunch gravel as stalkers assemble outside, chatting in Gaelic rhythms. The language is abandoned now, but its cadences remain. The ponies that will bring back the stags, slung across their backs, stamp and snuffle. The young ghillies who lead them, stalkers of the future, speak when spoken to, and not unless.

Then the start, with its changeless ritual. First, the greetings and the handshakes. Then the ceremony in which the "pieces", the Spartan food packets which last deerstalkers all day, are stowed in a saddle-bag. Most stalkers are tall men with long, elastic, ground-eating legs; their clients may be any shape or size; and the first mile is always ambled, so that breath can find its tempo and muscles warm up. It is interrupted, once. Somewhere the rifle is taken from its sleeve, and a sighting shot fired

at a chosen stone. The report flattens and echoes from the rocks around, shattering the lonely silence. Granite chips fly from the target stone. The ricochet bullet sings away into eternity. The breeze flicks away the reek of powder. The bolt comes back, the spent case slips backward from the breech. The stalker stoops, picks it up and pockets it. The rifle is sleeved again. The march resumes.

The glen, the braes, and the mountains round them go quiet once more. The small voice of a burn tinkling, and the wind which ruffles the heather, can be heard again as ears readjust after the violence of the shot. High up, miles away, as yet unseen, a stag whose last day has come lifts his head from the cotton grass. Perhaps he heard something, some small disturbance in his sound pattern where a man would have heard nothing at that distance; perhaps not. He has a few more hours; hours of which he will not know the ending; hours in which the stalkers will close in on him secretly, creeping through dead ground, outflanking the wind. And around him, all over half of Scotland, other stags will be left to make themselves heard.

Wreathed in the Wessex fog, I gather up my pigeons. The

spaniel brings in another which fell unseen. My thoughts are far away. In spirit I am listening. The roaring of the stags, that strange and thrilling sound, equalled only by the hunting horn in making the skin contract in answer to its thrills, will not be heard by me this year. But memory plays an encore, and across the years it comes again, as it did in the Cairngorms, Galloway, Monadliath, and the eerie spaces of Rannoch Moor, something heard wherever the red deer come, the commanding voice of the rut.

We talk of the roaring of the stags, but roaring it is not – to my ear, anyway. Though more prolonged, it is nearer to a cough or a bark, reminding me of a tiger, hidden in jungle but proclaiming his presence. Stags are not shy at such times, but are generally out of sight, which adds impact to the sound. The months of good living are ending. Vigour is at its height. Before the struggle for existence restarts, the future of the race must be ensured. Out of the mist a patriarch announces himself. His abrupt, compelling voice carries a message for all red deer, male or female. Life will now be renewed, on his terms. Those who think differently can try their luck against him. The roaring increases. Optimistic younger stags accept the challenge and say so. Roars which began wide apart draw closer together, like the approach to battle of medieval kings, heralded by trumpet blasts. Somewhere, in a corrie or fold in the hills, antlers clash in battle with the big stag's harem as the prize. The law of Nature, which preserves the strength of species, is that procreation is for the strong, and strength is tested every year.

FOUR hundred miles south the sunshine grows and breaks through. What began as a day for the gun develops into one for the rod. Although fishing is for me a sport of departed Summer, I take my fly tackle out again. The season for trout ended three weeks back, and now I go out for grayling, Britain's most under-rated game fish. A new age of enlightenment enables justice to be done to them at last.

Grayling, related to trout and salmon, come from the Arctic. Originally they colonised only rivers flowing into the North Sea. The isthmus which in pre-history joined Kent to Europe prevented them reaching the English Channel estuaries. But the old-time monks, who knew a thing or two about making life worth living, transplanted grayling eggs from Yorkshire into Wessex streams. This improved their menus in Lent, and perhaps their sport in the trout close season. But for the last hundred years, during which dry fly-fishing became something between a sport, an art and a social grace, grayling could be caught in Summer only, generally by anglers trying for trout. They considered grayling odious in comparison. No wonder, at that time of year. Grayling rise to flies as trout do, but they spawn in late Spring instead of Winter. So grayling in the Summer are in the same state as trout in January, or unmended salmon kelts, lean, feeble and unwholesome. How different in October.

Now they are silver, graceful, swift and muscular. The great sail-like fins above their backs are touched with vermilion. When fresh from the water they lace the air with the clean scent of thyme (their Latin designation is Thymulla). They have more names than almost any other fish, twenty-eight in France alone. In old times they were known in Britain as umber, meaning shadow. Purple-patch fishing writers called a grayling the lady of the stream.

Not all were as complimentary. H. T. Sheringham wrote a famous Malediction, beginning with the words, "I will write about graylings; I will vehemently abuse them." And others did just that, because they ceased to fish when the trout season ended, and never met grayling in their prime. Times have changed. Grayling in the Summer are no less of a nuisance than before, but grayling in the Autumn are recognised as one of life's boons. More and more fisheries now allow grayling fishing in Autumn and Winter where this does not interfere with the spawning trout, and I for one welcome grayling, whether in the river or on a plate, preferably smoked, as the trout's equal. In mainland Europe they are ranked superior.

The when and the where of it makes Autumn grayling fishing special. Fly-fishing is a physical sport; it keeps blood and muscles active, and the body warm in the cooler air. The sun which shines upon us now does not raise blisters, as it often does in trout time. It gilds the day, yet leaves it sharp and energising. All around, in work and sport, are signs of the year's most active phase.

Grayling are always in beautiful places. They need even purer water than trout. The streams that hold them are swift and clear, threading the Autumn pageant. Yellowing leaves of alder fall on the surface and are borne away like tiny gondolas as I knot-on a fly and watch for signs. The river weed is dying, and the great green underwater caverns are joined again into long glides with a quickening flow. The acceleration suits the grayling way of life. They do not lie high, like trout, sipping in the flies with minimum movement, but instead sweep upwards from depths where the eye cannot see, taking the fly at the high point of a long looping parabola.

Sometimes the fishing is all action. Grayling are not loners, as trout tend to be. They form shoals, and seem little bothered when one in their company is caught. Today I am either lucky or clever (it does not matter which) and take eight without walking more than fifteen yards. The breeze is upstream, just where I want it. In two hours it thins the foliage on the bankside trees, so that the view of the field beyond opens up. The plough is turning it from stubble-yellow to fertility-brown. The strip of furrows widens as the tractor comes and goes, a wheeling flock of seagulls in its wake like tattered papers whirled and tossing on the wind.

Knocking-off time is not far ahead for the tractor driver and for me. Another day of the ebbing year is nearly done. What remains of it is chilling off. No flies are hatching now, so I reel in for the last time. A small grayling follows my artificial fly as if about to take, thinks better of it, and lives to face another winter. The breeze has a sudden bitter tang, as appetising as good lager. An old man in a cottage garden behind me has lit a bonfire, and is forking on to it his day's haul of weeds. The homely English breath of Autumn blends with the first shades of twilight. I call to him. He comes to his gate, knocking out his pipe. We discuss his burn-off, and suspect a coming storm. I leave him with a brace of grayling.

"I see your rod bending quite a bit," he says. "Grey fish, eh? That's kind of you. They're good eating this time of year. Not many gentlemen know."

Gentlemen are not credited with knowing much, in the opinion of cottage garden veterans, especially those by riversides. I suspect this one has long since learned, in his own way, all about October grayling.

The months turn. A blend of the exuberant with the solemn introduces November. The opening meets are held, we get busy with the pheasants, the skies are lit to celebrate the deliverance of Parliament from an early remote control bomb, and we remember the Fallen. Those of us who can actually remember them – who they were, what they looked like, and how they fell – are fewer now, forty years on. I am one who can. For me the memorials in local churchyards and squares are not mere names in stone, their numbers the measure of each village's sacrifice. They are faces and voices, still alive to me, though they are dead. They bring back memories of scenes better not talked about. Better forgotten, say some; and very true, except for the small fact that to forget is possible only for those who were not there. Those of us who came back cannot discard from our thoughts the friends we left; to whom Fate denied a future; and who now live on in the minds of us, their comrades. Not forgotten is no empty phrase. We know that if shell or bullet had hit us and not them, they would have stood stiff-backed in our memory. Things being as they are, the duty falls to us.

But we do not do it alone. On this November day there is no generation gap. Looking at those around me I think how young some of them are, and remember how young we all were when, not caring much for philosophical small print but knowing the danger of the times, we left these Wessex scenes to defeat a threat to our country. We made our marks on it for each other. Unforgetting of the camp fire talk, I still pass pubs where drank my comrades who are dead, cottages where girl friends lived, brooks where trout were guddled, gardens which bore the print of hands long stilled, houses where women read telegrams which told them they were widows. The loss is with the living. The dead are spared the deprivation. "For them no more the blazing hearth shall burn," but they do not know.

Two minutes is enough. One can think much, remember much in that time, and those thoughts are my own. At Last Post I can face the world again. But I have never yet endured until the end of the Royal British Legion's broadcast from the Albert Hall. While my family watch, they cannot know my mind, and times come when I must top up the glasses to conceal my thoughts and, a little later, walk alone in the garden under the autumn stars. Stars are a soldier's friends. They, if nothing else, would be there again tomorrow, so one thought, on nights of battle, like Lord Ballantrae, marching across Burma in *Towards the East*:

> The jackals scream, the landmarks pass, the stages
>   Are made and drop behind;
> The stars that scan all warriors down the ages
>   Look on me and are kind –
> The soldier stars that scan the beats of heaven,
>   To whom all things are known;
> Who watch the fields where men of old have striven
>   And soon shall watch our own.

Most of us still wear our poppies when we arrive for the first big pheasant shoot. Autumn is dissolving into Winter, but the weather breaks in our favour. The day dawns lively and clear. Wind and sunshine keep things moving; tree-crowns rock; the lake ripples; everywhere an inter play of light and shade; the damp breath of fertility comes from acres sown to winter wheat. At quarter to ten, the scene set, every man and woman is in place.

WE face north. A long inward-curving wooded hill stretches forward on our right, ploughed fields and the lake to the left, beyond them pastures and more woods. Ahead, where trees cut off the view, the grey wall of a big house shows behind dark green cedars. Seven men and a lady are shooting today, and now moving to their pegs, the numbered wands which mark each gun's position. I am not one of them. I shall enjoy my role of beater more. Each to his taste. Mine is for sport on the move. Their day will be stationary. The beat will come in from the West, so they will be shooting up-sun, undazzled, and are doubtless duly thankful.

Game shooting is primarily a harvest, the gathering of a crop never more important than now in the economics of the land; secondly, it is enjoyment for those taking part. All harvests are cause for celebration, though only some are celebrations in themselves. To see corn cascading into a silo is a good sight for those who worked to put it there, and sets the tone for the feasting which follows. It is difficult to be similarly uplifted about harvesting sugar beet, an inhospitable task in the mud of the cold back-end, or about sending lambs to the slaughterhouse. But all these are among the varied culminations of human effort, and of the turning year. Since the gathering of the pheasants is also one of them, small wonder that people take pleasure in it.

Today's pleasure is being shared not only by the eight people with guns, but by fifty-six others, including me, all of us active participants in our different ways. As a mental exercise, while waiting for events to begin moving, I itemise this cross-section of countryfolk. The eight shooters are the owner of the big house, his son, two local farmers, a racing motorist, an athletic young woman barrister, a neighbouring peer, and somebody important in industry. Since many pheasants will be in the air together, fast shooting will often be needed. So each has two guns, and a loader in attendance. The loaders, an influential octet, sticklers for doing things in due form, comprise three neighbouring game-keepers, a garage proprietor, a postman, a shopkeeper, the butler from the big house, and a sergeant-major on leave. Five of the shooters are accompanied by their wives, one by his brother, one by his girl friend, one by her ten-year-old son. These supporters have subsidiary functions, forewarning of approaching birds, marking where they fall, keeping eyes on dogs, and ensuring the availability of cherry brandy and similar aids to concentration. Cynics say the latter predominates. So the eight-gun "line" is two dozen strong.

Behind the shooters, moving into position as I watch, five pickers-up are tactically placed far back, all with highly trained dogs. They are a retired colonel, a company director, the local probation officer, a university lecturer and a vet's wife. Not all the shot birds fall where the shooters can see them. Some fly on for several hundred yards before dropping; some are winged and unless promptly found will suffer and die, helpless victims of fox or stoat. After each drive the shooters' dogs gather the birds lying close to the gun line. The pickers-up, having watched the shooting, disappear into the hinterland to make the distant, difficult finds. Some birds will take an hour or more to bring to hand, and teamwork is needed to provide continued cover when the gun line moves on. There are to be six drives today. The five pickers-up have eleven dogs – three yellow labradors, two black labradors, three springer spaniels, a golden retriever, a flat-coated retriever, and a German short-haired pointer.

Where pheasants are many, driving is the most efficient way of shooting them. The shooters wait in position and the birds from wide strips of woodland are sent forward and over them. This is more difficult than it sounds. Game coverts are thick; undergrowth, especially if bramble, may be impenetrable by men; pheasants are cunning and their reaction to the approach of a man is not to fly, but to lie low and hidden until he has passed. So the beaters have been chosen for being pheasant-wise, with eyes sharpened for country and for cover, for being thorough in places where experience or instinct tell them birds may be lying. They are of all ages from schoolboys to spry septuagenarians. Most are local farm workers, knowing their land and its weather, and the ways of game birds in all variations. There are also three off-duty policemen, two schoolmasters, a merchant seaman, a docker, a concrete mixer. Not all are male. Two gamekeepers' wives are regulars. And there is a newcomer, my daughter, whose physical presence causes even her most senior colleagues to take a well-timed eyeful.

Twenty minutes ago they piled into a covered wagon. Later she told me that a time-honoured rural tradition had been observed. As she climbed in last of all, with the deference due by a novice in the presence of experts, a hidden voice up front rapped out, "Do your flies up, Fred." It had been easy to identify Fred. A fresh-faced youth with reddening cheeks stood grinding his teeth, his eyes on his boots as the wagon lurched away. Throughout the length of Britain, wherever a noticeable lady boards a beaters' wagon, the same words are uttered, in the cause of innocent merriment. Two under-keepers went with them, to control the drive. Soon they are a mile back, deployed along a ride, and waiting for the signal to start.

The morning turns quiet when they have gone. Shooters, time on their hands, chat in groups, or swivel around, eyes on the treeline, checking their surroundings, estimating distances. The wind sends showers of yellow leaves streaming over the furrows. There they will fall and rot, building future fertility. Higher than the leaves, going further, sycamore keys are whirling, like flights of tiny helicopters. Where the furthest leaves fall, the keys have not lost height and go spinning on. Thinking of aircraft turns the calendar back fifty years; momentarily there are no noises in the sky, only the traffic on a big road two miles off. All else is peace.

Enter six hale and weather-beaten senior citizens, three at each end of the gun line. They toddle circumspectly, men accustomed to the full glare of public attention, and bearing rolled flags as insignia of office. They are the stops. At eighty, a stop is in his prime. The aura of long years of sport surrounds them. Is it fanciful to seem to hear, fitting in this English scene, *The Boys of the Old Brigade*? They deserve a marching song. In this land of free speech their opinions, though sibyline with tact and muffled by local accent, will not be hushed up. Each has inherited, by natural succession and increasing immobility, his own particular tree at every drive throughout the day. At the foot of it he will exercise the skills which, when his hour is come, lift a good stop above the level of ordinary humanity.

Guns are the soloists, and stops the first violins in the orchestra of the shoot. The beaters give the impetus to the drive, the stops shape it, funnelling the pheasants towards the guns by stick-tapping, fortissimo to diminuendo as developments demand, or well-timed flicks of their flags.

The head keeper, his briskness expressing the mounting expectancy, joins me. We move away together, two spaniels at my heel, along the woodside where the beaters went. He has the air of a youngish conductor about to mount his rostrum, and is girt about with scientific gadgetry; a two-way radio, microphone clipped to his lapel, binoculars, a hunting horn. After half a mile we stop.

"Start from here," he says, "wait until the beat comes past you, then come along with them and work your dogs just short of the left-hand beater." He slips into the wood and blows his horn to start the drive. The day, as distinct from daylight, has begun.

Between me and the gun line, the woodside up which we have walked has a rampart of thick brambles. They have choked and overgrown a deer-leap, dug here as an estate boundary by some beneficiary of the battle of Hastings. Now they form a half-mile no man's land, impervious to beaters and their sticks, but not to pheasants or to spaniels. The advancing beat will send many pheasants running downhill into the brambles. Posy and Poppy, bright-eyed and smiling at action stations, watching me for the order of release, are experts at evicting pheasants from such places. But there is longer to wait.

Soon after the horn's soft note has died I sense that the beaters are moving – sense, not hear, for at first there are no sounds. But the silence changes its texture, then is no longer total. Something, perhaps many things, are disturbing it but cannot be detected yet, as when a water surface ruffles before one feels the wind. This is not an estate where men shout or make the whirring noises by which beginners at beating try to prove that they know their stuff. The only sound effects here are rattled sticks. At first I do not hear even these. But somebody else does, and raises the voice which heralds more pheasant drives than not.

> A blue uneasy jay was chacking,
> A swearing screech, like tearing sacking.

The tell-tale of the woods broadcasts his message, as Masefield heard him in *Reynard the Fox*. Nothing can happen without a jay knowing it, and therefore the whole world soon knowing it, too. The news spreads. Then follows the procession which is the great fringe-benefit of a shooter's day. Ahead of the beat, the life of the wood is on the move.

The first signs are at tree-top height. Woodpigeons clapper out, making as much fuss as possible. They circle, check what is going on, then set off for somewhere more tranquil to preen their feathers and coo and gurgle. A scattering of long-tailed tits comes through, unhurried and happy, their small talk busy, silhouetted amid the lacework of twigs and branches between me and the sky. At ground level a heavy body crashes. A deer has started up suddenly, and clumsily, then finds her bearings and is gone. A green woodpecker, crimson crowned, threads his bouncing flight between the trees, an exotic figure against the sober English colours. The rattle of sticks is audible now, and coming nearer.

Blackbird after blackbird prinks – their pitch rising, the clamour growing. Chaffinches join in. This is more than alarm. Their indignation suggests major scandal. The cause soon appears. A tawny owl, rudely awakened in daylight, flies soft-winged through the wood, heavy-headed and portentous, mobbed by the noisy rabble all around him, but fearing to come too close. He veers right-handed, and the tumult fades away. Something moves on an ash bole and resolves itself into a tree-creeper, mouse-like as it runs up among the branches. At knee height to me a little party of wrens flit modestly past and disappear into some dead willowherb. Pheasants' feet patter on dead beech leaves, telling me that some are already infiltrating the brambles in front. From the gun line a single shot, disruptive and isolated, punctuates a scene now reduced to whispers. Then the urgent sound of somebody running. An underkeeper, carrying a furled flag at the trail, slips nimbly out of the covert, through the brambles behind me, and takes post as flanker on the plough.

The diligent sticks are nearly abreast of us. Beyond some ivy, trailing from an oak tree, I see the left hand beater – one of the policemen, an old hand at the game. He lifts his cap to declare himself; I lift mine in acknowledgment. He moves on, tapping methodically. When I can see the broad of his back it is time to go.

Two spoken names, two pointings of the hand, start Posy and Poppy toward their spheres of influence. They are skilled operators, full of game sense and gun sense, some of it taught, most of it inherited. They have different styles and methods. Poppy, a springer, puts her head down and charges the thorns like a rugby forward pitching into a ruck. Posy, a cocker, eels her way in like an enlarged weasel, with which she has other temperamental similarities. In truth it is they, not I, who have been invited to the shoot. Their attributes combine to make them an effective brace – the honest grafting of the springer, the cocker's determination and intuitive flair, the self-restraint of them both.

Ahead is half a mile of thick and thorny cover with every twenty yards or so a pheasant lying, tucked in between tussocks of dead grass under the brambles, invisible a foot away, detectable only by scent. The spaniels' task is to put them into the air, high up over the guns, not all together in a flock but in steady progression which will give the shooters a chance at each. Every square yard under the brambles must be explored. If even one pheasant is seen to fly out behind us, it will be a black mark.

So I myself move slowly, a dog hunting hard on each side, missing no ground, crossing in front of me, confirming each other's ground. A good spaniel first locates the pheasant, by nose not by accident, then closes-in on it from the direction which will send it towards the guns, and finally puts it up with such thrust and decision that the bird launches itself steeply into the air, as is off a springboard, instead of flying away low. In order to flush them forward, my dogs do not move far ahead of me, but go wide to each flank. The wind is towards us, blowing the scent of pheasants into their nostrils. They must not yield to temptation and be drawn forward by this. If they do so, they may unknowingly pass other pheasants behind them and, disturbing them from the wrong side, send them back over me instead of forward over the guns.

The first find is slow in coming. Then, to a crash of splintered underbrush, Poppy pushes one out on the far left. It is a hen and breaks towards the plough. The flank flag winks, just once but in time, and turns her. Thirty seconds later another single shot tells me that we have put that one into the bag.

Now the birds sent forward by the beat are concentrating forward, the climax approaching. Some of them plane away, swerving adroitly between the trees, coming down short of the stops; others foot it, and join them there. The controlled movement of the beat builds up the pressure. The stops, calculating their moment, reveal their presence. Then, for the pheasants, it is suddenly wings or nothing and everybody is in action together – beaters, stops, shooters, loaders, and spectators.

Back in the brambles we have our build-up, too. Some pheasants lose their nerve and run ahead instead of lying low, so the volume of pheasant-scent wafting back to the dogs continually increases. But they must not let it distract their attention from the thorough search for those that sit tight. One by one these

161

rocket into the air. I count fifteen forward for only two back, and am well aware that our host and the headkeeper will have counted them too. Even so there are twenty more in the final ten paces of the brambles when we get there, so the three shooters on the right of the line have a lively finale.

Again, the horn's soft note. Guns are broken and unloaded, beaters push their way from covert, thorns rasping on oilskins, pickers-up stride off, shooters and their companions gather the nearby bag, two spaniels stand blown and grinning, convinced of their part as architects of success, but not so blown that they are not ready and willing to help in the pick-up. Host and keepers hold a tactical inquest. And out come the stops quacking their observations like elderly mallard.

"Lordy were getting 'em," says one. "Stood need to," another declares, "I send 'un some lovely birds."

Two new figures make their appearance. The game cart moves out from the background, its custodian and its driver obvious men of consequence. They go from peg to peg picking up the kill, sorting it into braces of cock and hen, hanging them on cross-poles according to grade, keeping their own counsel about the pegs where game was properly shot and where it was not.

The pegs, the business end of a formal shoot, the ultimate factor in its success, are for those privileged on the day. Sometimes I am invited, and sometimes to decline would be churlish, but when I find myself thus favoured, waiting for the birds to come over, my feelings are those of being in the wrong place. Eyes front, listening for the sound of wings, I sit on my stick. An inner voice asks, What are you doing here? I feel like answering, What, indeed?

There are many ways of enjoying shooting, and the waiting game is not for me. It is for those whose main interest is in the gun, its skilful use the attraction. Mine is in the wider scene, including the birds themselves, and especially the art of the dog. Those to whom a peg is paradise regard these things as subservient to marksmanship. No skin off their noses; it is for the good of all that somebody should. But to me the marksmanship and the kill, though undoubtedly the culmination, are subservient to

the things which make them possible. When, loaded and ready, I hear the beaters working towards me, hear the cries of "Mark!" "Hen forward!" "Cock, right!" I know that my natural place is not where I am, but with them.

If I kill, and I have no objection to doing so, I prefer the deed to be my own effort, not the finishing touch to those of others. At the end of the day I like to know that my legs and lungs have been in action, not merely my shoulder. At its start I like to see the ground ahead and all around untouched by human foot; willows and the white grass of Winter bowing to the wind, the black leafless thorn hedges standing stiff, green bramble and the darker green of gorse, flash of water behind reeds, rough shaws, some spinneys, and rews where real skill is needed to push a pheasant out.

Such is the rough shooter's scene, best shared by half a dozen friends, only half of whom are human, where sport is self-made by eye and country know-how, and where we take what comes, in the chance of the moment. Nothing is laid out in advance to make it easy. We shall not need a game cart. We carry. And if the game-bag strap is pulling as the day wears on, it will be in response to the variety which is the spice of rough-shooting. A brace of pheasants, a hare, some rabbits, a partridge and a snipe, a pigeon or two, a woodcock with luck, and some duck to end

the day would be perfection if I could say, "All my own work." To have been helped would halve the contentment.

Why call it rough? I do not know. There is nothing rough about it, but much precision and care. On the other hand, it can hardly be called smooth; so there, perhaps, is the explanation. But fundamental to it is the fact that we rough-shooters, still following the sport as it was in muzzle-loading days, are the heirs and successors of those who named thousands of inns the Dog and Gun, but very few the Gun and Dog. The priority speaks for itself.

Dog-and-gun men prefer to be mobile. If the favoured few are enjoying themselves as much as I am, they cannot hope for more. Other drives follow, then we break for lunch. A pale sun shines on men exchanging friendly insults, and on women sharpening their repartee. Posy and Poppy, whose mileage in twisting, turning and doubling about through thorns and bracken must now be in the teens, are resting in the car.

To their disgust they are replaced in the afternoon by Hazel and Spark, specially chosen for the declared agenda. There will be only two drives. From the first of them many pheasants will fall into, or beyond, the river; and it is a big river. Hazel, a springer, is headstrong – sometimes careless – on land, but a renowned performer in water. In her five seasons she has swum this river hundreds of times, often in flood, and few of her return journeys have been unburdened. Spark, a cocker, is eleven years old, her sight failing, legs and wind not what they were. But she knows this shoot as well as the oldest beater, and the last drive will end at a place where Spark has become an honoured name. When, for her, it has become a case of "once more into the breach dear friend," a high moment for the shooters will be no more.

There, in due course, we arrive. Our position in the beat is carefully calculated to bring us this precise position. Hazel, four more voyages to her credit warms up and dries off, questing in and out of rhododendrons and laurel, then comes to heel for the last 150 yards. They end at a cliff top above a quarry, on the floor of which the guns are placed. The cliff's lip curls over in a hanging strip about six yards deep and forty yards wide, unsafe for men to go, covered by heather and low-lying bramble, over a drop of about seventy feet. The pheasants which legged-it in front of the beat are now hidden there. The nearest stop estimates forty.

I put a lead on Hazel, whose intervention at this stage would be disastrous. This is where subtlety is worth more than enthusiasm. Spark sniffs around, her tail going. She knows where she is. What must not happen now is that all the birds should flush together. One or two of the stops, who have seen it all before, wander over. "We don't want one of them hoorooshes," remarks one veteran, as if I did not know. I sit on a log, the same old log year after year, where the lip protects me from shot from below. Spark, on the lip's slope, is dropped at the downwind end, tasting the air. With all the wiliness and general savvy of the cocker race, she takes special pride in tickling them out two or three at a time; the other cocker characteristic of not being a fool will keep her from falling over the edge. Her eyes, though dim, still focus on me, waiting for the signal.

The headkeeper arrives, walks to the edge and peers over, then gives me the nod. I say, "Gently Spark, push 'em up." Her nose had told her where the nearest birds lie. She evicts three, sees enough to watch one crumple in the air and fall out of sight into the quarry, then looks back at me. "Go on," I say. Two more airborne, I say "Hup"; she waits for the word to continue. And so, yard by yard, we clear the lip, as we have done for seasons past. The old lady comes happily back, bringing with her a gundog's greatest reward, knowledge of a job well done. I tickle her neck. The old stop pats her and says "Good 'un, that!" She does not know what the words mean, but they are music in her ears.

The horn again; this time it ends the day. The pickers-up bring in the last birds. Round the game cart all and sundry, old and young, rich and poor, lean on sticks, puff out smoke, reminisce, joke, ask questions, look forward to the next time, and disperse their various ways. The picture is one of arrested motion at the end of the social revolution.

An Earl on his Acres

An earl stands on his ancestral acres, his son and heir beside him. His guests, one way and another, have financed his day's shooting, or most of it. The keepers, the loaders, the beaters and the stops, who are paid for their efforts, are his henchmen, in lineal succession to the diggers of the deer-leap now under the brambles nine centuries later; those of them who live on the estate think of it as theirs. The pickers-up, who are not paid except for a grace-and-favour brace of pheasants each, are his minor leiges. The English genius for constructing class distinctions, and then ignoring them, remains intact – here, out of doors, in the evening, under the English sky, in the name of sport. The ancient trees, the soft earth, the reek of leaves rotting, the rising mist, the coming night, wrap us all in English weather, and in the English scene. We know our ground; in our various ways, we stand our ground; we do not readily give away much of our past.

Outside the estate saw-mill a wide grass space gives turning circles to timber-bogies off-loading their cargoes here in felling time. Ten minutes ago it was a car park. Now, in the dusk, mine is the only car remaining. Everybody else has filtered away by lanes and paths into the countryside from which they concentrated for the day's sport. The shooters, their loaders and their supporters are back at the house for tea and leave-taking. The keepers went with them, to supervise the cleaning of the guns, and to be suitably enriched. The pickers-up, always the last to return to base, brought in the final birds, rubbed down their tired dogs, and drove off. The game-cart rumbled away behind its lurching tractor, up the tree-lined drive towards the larder. By car or bicycle or on foot, the beaters and the stops made for home as soon as they were paid; most to villages where lights are already glowing behind curtained windows, some to isolated cottages from which stockmen tend outlying steadings, some to nearby towns. The sound of their voices, by ceasing, changes the small world they have left. Behind them the by-ways and the short-cuts through the woods revert to a silence safe enough for rabbits to come out and feed, and for deer to pass wraith-like to the fields. Even the roads are lonely, for this is tea-time, on a

Saturday, in winter, the end of the active day, and two hours before spruced-up masculinity heads out to the pubs, leaving women and children to the television. Our last rites take longer than those of others.

The four spaniels wait behind the car, watching me while I change boots for slippers, and my jacket for the much-worn duffle coat which has seen me home from woods, moors and riversides across more than twenty years. My daughter makes coffee, well-earned by those who have walked and brushed the woods all day. The morning's dogs stretch their legs after three hours rest, the afternoon brace lie tired but happy waiting for the signal to enter the travelling box. Steam from the coffee floats in the chill air of evening; here in the shelter of a belt of holly trees, their berries reddening towards Christmas, mist is forming and no wind disperses it.

In the fading light cock pheasants call, each announcing his return to home ground where he will roost or jug for the night. After a day's shooting which has seen the fall of more than two hundred of his kind, the peace of the coverts reasserts itself, and life goes on unaltered without residue of fear. The spaniels listen, set their ears, but make no move. Each has spent half a day hunting pheasants, ejecting them from hiding into the air, marking them down, finding them, retrieving them, their minds on little else except pheasants. But, now the day is over, pheasants are no longer their concern, just part of the world around them. Even when one of them, brassy-looking and brazen-voiced, sprints over the grass ten yards away, heading for the warmth of a laurel clump, he is treated with detachment – something to look at, but now no longer a cause for action.

Some scientists maintain that the animal brain cannot reason, but operates only on the level of signals and reactions, every regular stimulus arousing its own particular response by reflex, regardless of circumstance. People who think this cannot know much about their subject, though their qualifications, veterinary and otherwise, may convince them that they do. It is obvious that animal intelligences vary in degree and character, as human intelligence does; in some species the memory dominates, in others reasoning modifies it. Nobody can doubt the animal capability for constructive thought in dealing with unexpected situations if he has had contact with dogs, horses, cats, pigs, sheep, goats, rats, mice, hedgehogs, moles, stoats, weasels, hares, foxes or badgers in their natural environments; what happens in the artificial settings of laboratories is another matter. Birds are also another matter. Being warm-blooded reptiles, they consolidated their evolution much earlier than mammals, and have changed little since. Even so, I do not believe they are automata, as some academics would have us believe. Certainly spaniels know when work has finished.

When it is time to go, each of them waits to be ordered in by name, then jumps over the tail-gate into the travelling box. Before the clutch is let in, they have curled themselves into a mutually supportive pattern and are falling asleep. The car radio crackles into life. The weather man's voice comes sharp on cue. A change is on the way. The night will be clear and still, the temperature sinking into frost as a high pressure area develops to the west. This will "pull in" northerly winds tomorrow, bringing the first snow of Winter to high ground, cold rain elsewhere. Forewarned, we drive home through lanes over which the moon and stars are riding high, throwing sharp-edged shadows on the fields. Soon I alone am awake.

The driving seat window is open a slit. The outer air drifts in, bringing the tang of rotting leaves. The full force of vegetative life, which yeasted up in Spring as greenery, then ripened into Autumn fruits, is sinking back to the earth whence it came, richer for the sunshine which it has absorbed, ready to rise again as sap next year. To stand in a wood now, with night intensifying the senses, would be to hear what at present I can only smell, whispers and rustlings stealing into what at first seems total silence. These are not the sounds of animate life, but of leaves falling and touching twigs and branches as they go. Weakened and dry, their anchorages are broken by the thrust of next year's developing buds, and they part from their trees, falling softly but not unheard to the woodland floor. Every hour or so, intensifying the gentle rhythm, comes a pattering sound, like a rain shower; an ash tree, as its habit, is releasing its leaves in batches. Occasionally a plop signals a falling acorn.

The living woods are always stirring. Inside the car, I do not get the message. Overhanging boughs enclose the swish of the tyres and the purr of the engine, drowning all else. Only occasional gear changes, and halts and pull-aways at a crossroads, punctuate the journey. A mile from home, there is a sudden stirring in the dog box; the deep and leisured breathing breaks up into yawns and snuffles of wakefulness. I know that four pairs of eyes are alert, watching through the rear window for landmarks in the outer dark. It is always thus, a return to consciousness a mile out, whichever way I come. The smell of the land through the window slit may have brought awareness; so may familiar sequences of turnings and gradients. Whatever it is, the cause cannot be dismissed as "instinct" or "bump of location"! The fact is that dogs' minds can relate happenings to sequels, and work things out.

In their kennels in the barn they curl up in golden straw to sleep for two more hours before they eat. Time has settled my own programme. Outer clothes are hung in the boiler room; tea and toast restore enough energy for me to read the mail and the morning newspapers, which arrived after we had left; then a long hot bath, and dinner.

Beyond the curtained windows a winter night is deepening. The promised frost bites harder. Here, under soft lights, and coffee and port beside me, out of doors seems more than a mere wall's width away. Some people might think it uninviting, but I have not done with it yet. In due course I don coat and cap and go to say Goodnights.

Eight bright eyes reflect the light when I switch on; four tails thump. But no dog moves to touch nose on hand at their kennel doors. They are too comfortable. Outside, the frost smells keen but in the stables it is only a distant rumour, full of the clean warmth of healthy horses. One stands blanketed and prick-eared on his bed of shavings; when I reach up to pull his ear he gives me a friendly biff in the chest with his nose. His companion in the next box has no time for frivolity. In plain horse language she says "Don't bother me, I'm eating hay," and pulls another fid from the net. I leave her to it. The Plough, Orion, Lyra, Cassiopea, the Swan and the other constellations are glinting now. The icy air sharpens their pin-points overhead. Nature is turning the screw. What matter? In my small area of responsibility man and maid and horse and dog will all sleep snug to-night.

WE wake to a well rimed Sunday morning. Then the wind rises, and the words of the forecaster are fulfilled. The first scattering of rain meets us at the church door, cutting short the parson's valedictions and sending the congregation to their cars at the double. By lunch time the northerly is driving a downpour across the windows in horizontal slashes. The sky is dark and full of mischief. Beneath it, the storm marches across the downs in grim majesty as curtains of rain come sweeping through. It is a day for keeping under cover, and for estimating tomorrow's prospects. Small matter nowadays if they are no better.

Modern clothing is one of the twentieth century's boons. In the nineteenth, things were very different. Any photograph or painting of the time proves the point. At shooting parties, every man was cloaked or coated in stiff serge or heavy tweed, as encumbered as knights in armour; horse-and-carriage drivers and

171

outer passengers were encased in felt to contain warmth and resist rain. Yet to be cold, or wet, or unduly restricted, or merely uncomfortable is virtually impossible nowadays, come hurricane, come cloud-burst, let alone the normal hazards. We now wear quilted clothing, as the mongolians of high Asia have done for centuries. It took the Korean war to persuade western participants that the Chinese were sensibly dressed after all. Since then life in winter has taken more turns for the better.

Insulation is more important than weight in retaining warmth. We now apply the principle of captive air pockets to light-weight waterproof fabrics and feel as if we walk on air, even when fully protected. Zip-fasteners or press-studs are more efficient than buttons in effecting leak-free closure. We have solved the problems, which defied our ancestors, of preventing wind blowing up our sleeves, of making collars weather-proof, and of totally water-resistant boots. A man whose neck, hands and feet are warm is a fair way of being warm all over, so we dress accordingly. Moreover, what we wear looks increasingly attractive, as well as sporting and tidy. There is no longer any reason why shooting people should resemble guerrilla-fighters on the losing side, though some still do.

Nevertheless, most of us have a recurrent feeling that we ought "to be as our fathers were, in the days 'ere we were born", that we are somehow wanting in manhood because we do not share at least some of their discomforts. In my case this misgiving applies especially to rubber boots. Not that I would dream of wearing anything else, but an after-taste of forgotten guilt attaches to my doing so. Rubber boots are substantially older than I am, but my family debated their viability for a decade or two of my early life before deciding to give them a trial, and it was my own generation who finally conceded that they are the optimum choice for life as it now is.

Far away and long ago, in terms of time and change rather than distance, yeomen in Shropshire could not be convinced that anything could replace leather. Rubber "draws the feet", they said; as indeed it does, while also keeping them dry. Their arguments were manifold. Leather was natural. So boots were naturally made of leather, always had been, always would be. Leather was waterproof, if properly dubbined. It still is, if properly dubbined. But who does the dubbining? Nobody mentions knife boys.

Nowadays, this term describes a particular form of young delinquent. Between the wars it indicated the lowest form of domestic life in country households. Theoretically a knife boy cleaned knives for his first two years after leaving school, but this duty was likely to be cursory and infrequent. In fact, he cleaned the oil lamps that lit most farmhouses, and he dubbined boots, a long drawn-out and not displeasing process for those with time as well as boots on their hands. Now knife boys are no more, and in part consequence our life style has become so compressed time-wise that to dubbin our own boots is not an option. With sincere thanks to Providence I squirt hose-water over mine of the rubber variety, rendering them speckless in thirty seconds instead of the hour-long process of dubbining, not to mention the drying out.

As November nears its end, Winter takes over. The laden skies drop rain day after day. Fields which the ploughs have left, their work done, gleam wet. Some are already greened by the first spears of winter corn. From now on the common denominator of country life is mud. The mud that anchors cars in gateways, halts tractors, and stops tanks in battle, now decelerates the pace of the land. It reverts to what it was in the days of horse power, reminding us feelingly of the varied soil beneath our feet. They sink ankle-deep into the red loams of the West, squelch and suck through the Midland clay, and step buoyantly on the sands of Surrey and the lighter land in East Anglia and the Fens. In Wessex we slip and slide, demonstrating the weakness of our mortal nature by not always being able to stand upright. Chalk, when soaked, is as precarious as a ski slope.

The country colours fade into suspended animation. The lifeless grass turns pale. What looks like grey foam lies along the tops of leafless hedges; traveller's joy has changed into old man's beard. Any brighter patches hold the eye a furlong off; fox-red stems of dogwood above a water-logged ditch, the brave bright green of sallow. Naked branches open up the view. From the wrong side of a spinney I can see the pied and moving specks which are a distant pack of hounds, and their huntsman's red coat. They are working out a stale scent across the opposite hill, speaking to it dubiously, calling each other for second opinions. Then they check. A burst land drain is spilling a fan of flowing water across a concreted farm vehicle park. The fox has very sensibly run through it and over an open silage clamp beyond, foiling the line. The hunt stops, giving a chance for me, and others on foot, to catch up. The riders walk their horses round, dismount to stretch their legs, and some opportunists disappear to the far side of a Dutch barn. By the foxhunters' code it is made plain that this, and this alone, is for men only. The other lot can have the rest of England.

The strength of the fox's position is obvious. Those not in the know might sympathise with him in being outnumbered by the hounds thirty to one. Doubtless he is glad to be so. It is a clear case of the superiority of the individual over the committee when quick decisions have to be made. The fox has made his. The Hunt has not. Talk replaces action. The hounds cast themselves industriously, catch shreds of scent, acknowledging them with quivering yelps. Others dash to the latest finder, fail to own the line, try somewhere else at random, and confidence sinks to zero. Riders move to a safe range, away from the wind. Flasks are up-ended, some eat sandwiches. Most of us air opinions. The huntsman looks daggers.

If the hounds are barren of ideas where the fox has gone, all the men and women present have theirs, all different. Locals from the farm are in no doubt. "''E go that way every morning," they declare, pointing in three directions. The huntsman stops his low-pitched, beguiling, incomprehensible hound-talk and touches his horn. He has given them a fair chance, as he had to do; now he gives them a lead. When they flock to him he takes them off the concrete, round and beyond the silage clamp, out of the windflow with its piquant reek. His voice again, "Ai, ai, ai. Ai, little bitches. Find 'im then. Ai, ai, find me Charlie, find me Charlie ... Charlie ... Charlee ..."

The pasture here is foiled by sheep, but only paddock-wide. A few hounds cast boldly on and under a fence to an empty field. Their voices are blown back with the ring of certainty. The huntsman gallops to them, gathering hounds and calling "Yoo-ee, yoo-ee". Their music crashes out, rolling across the hills like church bells. They are away again; the horn doubles. The crafty few riders who had foreseen what would happen go with them, dwindling to black and scarlet dots. The rest, caught coffee-housing, cram together at a gap; those in front want daylight, those behind want haste; four-letter words lace the English air. We on foot are left alone, under a sky of grey clouds flying and a chill wind blowing.

In past years to be so left would have seemed an unkind fate to me. Once I rode to hounds and now do not; though the old fever remains in my blood the old compulsion has mellowed. The sound of the horn, that soft thin wail, has me moving towards it no matter what activity it interrupts. I could no more ignore it than I could talk during Beethoven's Ninth Symphony. It has

not yet brought me from my bed, as Peel's horn brought John Woodcock Graves, if only because I am not in bed at the time of day when foxes are being hunted (I wonder why he was). But sometime in the far future it might happen. The unexpected truth remains that, when those in the saddle are gone away, I feel no deprivation. The reasons lie in things as they are, not as they were.

That queue at the gap expresses the difference between the countryside in which I grew up and the one I live in now. Broadly speaking, the scenes, the places, the names, the people are the same. It is details which escape passers-by, but not those whose feet are on the ground, which accumulate to separate then from now. In this case the hedges start the chain reaction. Because hedges are no longer made to grow into stock-proof barriers, but must be stock-proof nonetheless, they are increasingly reinforced by barbed wire. Because barbed wire running through a hedge is invisible, at least to those approaching at speed, it is certain disaster and possible death to horse and rider. Therefore farmers leave artificial gaps containing jumpable barriers, so that the Hunts can pass.

But such gaps and jumps are necessarily narrow. Few can be taken more than three abreast, so in effect the mounted field goes over in line astern, stringing out the hunt, reducing the element of 'us', an all-together band of friends with each worth the place that he can get. Where we, in our day, could broaden our front, choose our line or whom to follow, and take whatever lay ahead, the present generation must wait their turn – not always, but too often to leave the underlying spirit unchanged. There is no place like a Hunt jump for establishing a pecking order, which is not at all the same concept as a place in the hunt.

Good luck to those whose elation at the soft horn's message takes them to the place in the queue. They are as cheerful, and in the case of the ladies as pretty, as those I remember. If they include some of my family, but not me, I am not complaining. Few of them know, and none need care, that things are not as they used to be at that moment when the stirrup cups are handed back, the Master gives the nod, the whipper-in leads the way, and the huntsman calls "Hounds, gentlemen, please." The words are as they always were, the facts another difference. "Hounds, ladies" would be more applicable now.

Breathes there a man with soul so dead that he regards this particular change as wholly adverse? I doubt it. If foxhunting now is in spirit what foxhunting was, its attractions for many will have much increased. Turning away from the hunt jump, scene of so much endeavour, manoeuvre and force of personality, I walk the four miles back to the village wondering where that cheerful company has gone, taking with them their talk and laughter, smell of horse sweat and cut turf, where they will finish, how their day will end. The last hour of a hunting day can be as rewarding as its start. When, as often, it has the virtue of solitude, it leaves a longer memory. The ending of my final day stays as fresh in mine as if it were happening now, not years ago.

The light is ebbing, as hounds throw up their heads at a double hedge, in the Midlands, north of the Trent. Scent sometimes lies well in the evening chill, sometimes fails completely. Now they are announcing failure. A voice says, "About enough, I think." Healthily tired, I do not at first recognise it as the Master's. Something still more authoritative follows. The horn has a message more final than I know. The huntsman blows Going Home.

The whippers-in count hounds, totting them in couples. A young man, red-faced and with his tie awry, trots up with two mud-spattered girls, all their horses blown. The Master says, "Anybody else?" The young man answers, "Nobody behind us, I think. We shut the gates." The huntsman reports, "All on, sir."

The Master calls, "This way then, everybody. They'll bring the boxes to the green." Loose-reined now, and at a walk, we come down from the windy hill. Spread below us in panorama is the eternal English evening. Shadows are growing out of hedge-rows and on the edge of woods. Skeletonic trees, half faded on the sight, loom up like ghosts. A group of great yews, a thousand years old, men say, darken quicker than the sun sinks and now

177

stand black as night. Where the valley levels out a pearly mist is forming. Black bullocks, made small as moles by distance, follow a man who pitches hay from a moving trailer. Down the hill, down a rew in dusk so deep between hazel brakes that I sense rather than see the horse in front, along a made lane into the vale and round several bends, until there ahead are the outlines of the horse-boxes and cattle trucks, square and blocky amid the curves of Nature, parked around a green on which a hamlet centres.

Drivers have lowered the ramps. Some interiors are lit by the soft radiance of hurricane lamps, in others torch beams sway. There are sounds of activity and subdued voices from riders who arrived there before us; horse talk as saddles come off and rugs go on, soft cursing, the sound of a bottle being opened. Hoofs thud on barred floors. The first engine starts, the first Good-byes – including mine. No box for me, I am less than an hour from stable, and shall hack home.

Winter's pervasive dampness hardens into frost. The sound of shod feet on the high road is suddenly crisper. On a hunter whose weakness is playing up at traffic I trot on to cut the time before a turning leads into quiet lanes with wide grass verges on which any drama can be played out. No vehicle passes before we reach it. Blackbirds are finding their roosts at shoulder level in an overgrown hedge, scarcely visible now. The first star appears. Between me and it the last starlings swing over in silhouette, partridge-like on their stiff-held wings, to tuck up for the night in ivy which clads a tall oak. Oncoming lights ahead.

Damnation. The evening bus which links the farms and villages along the byways is heading down this one towards me, its great unblinking headlights staring. I hook my fingers under the martingale strap, by way of precaution, swing on to the grass and trot on again to indicate determination. The bus comes inexorably towards us, a rumbling and roaring monster with a bellyfull of illumination, casting shadows which career and dance as if the world itself were rocking. Between blinks at the headlights I see two well cocked ears, as of a horse plotting some special piece of private entertainment, and seeing a heaven-sent excuse for it. Condensation inside the bus has steamed up its windows, so that they give out an orange glare as it comes abreast. For two seconds the bus's heat and light and roar and smell obliterate all else, as if the gates of hell had opened; then its dazzle and its thunder and its snorting exhaust are behind, not beside us, and anti-climax breaks.

With level and unbroken stride the horse under me heads calmly home. In daylight there would have been the devil to pay. There are priorities in horses' lives as well as in ours. He knows where his stable is, and that in the stable will be a bowl of bran, mashed with a bottleful of Guinness. Frivolities can wait tonight. Tomorrow is another day. Ice is forming on the puddles where I dismount in the yard. I see him to bed. But I never rode him again. There came a call to other matters, a trumpet instead of a horn. Before the next season the nations were fighting.

THE winds through which hounds hunt the fox grow ever colder now. Far away, far beyond Herma Ness on furthest Shetland, the weather gods of the North are brewing up their mischief and blow the first puffs of it southward on to us. It is the breath of icefields and frozen seas, the polar forces breaking out again. Ahead of these forewarnings come birds from moors and tundra which will be uninhabitable in Winter's full cold blast. The Arctic thrushes, fieldfares and redwings, moved in weeks ago. Now their flocks fly over the house each dusk when they leave the downs for shelter in the valley, a grating jabber from the fieldfares, and whispers from the redwings.

Golden plover came soon after them, travelling from their breeding areas in Scotland and briefly colonising their usual fields before flying on to estuaries on the Channel shore. The way they whistle on the wing tells us of their arrival before we see them, their liquid calling to each other as they forage tells us where to look. Their favourite staging posts are on arable land where the furrows are clay, rich in the larvae and molluscs on which golden plover live. Their choice reflects both force of habit and the course of history. Only some of the clay fields attract them; others which look as promising do not. Most of the ground they visit has been ploughed for centuries; they seem unaware of that which has been cultivated only since power-farming opened up slopes which horse and ox teams could not tackle. Often the plovers' fields were part of medieval strip cultivation. Six centuries past, perhaps earlier, the flocks had decided their migration routes; despite all the changes in the face of Britain, they have not been altered since.

The world's face – air, sea and land alike – is a network of long-established travel networks. The species which use them are those which arrive and leave punctually; swallows, cuckoos, warblers and fly-catchers in Summer, northern thrushes in Winter. Others change their ground only when hard weather impels them, moving from place to place haphazard, arriving any time. Now I am waiting for the siskins which in Wessex are heralds of real wrath to come, moving southwards with the snow at their tails. Both they and the golden plover bring the touch of Scotland with them. We heard the plovers lilting from rough ground on Strathspey, near where the corncrake rasped in the dusk; and we saw the siskins flitting at the edges of nearby pine woods, the cock birds giving their dark branches a flash of gold.

Here in southern England the night comes when I hear the wild geese go over. From the outer darkness, stealing-in on the senses, come the hound-like voices from the sky, travelling fast. White fronts throw their tongues like foxhounds, barnacles like beagles, pinkfoot and bean geese gruff as bloodhounds. I have heard them in various places in war and peace; when helmeted and silent, waiting for the invasion; moving out, through slippery inky gutters, to meet a morning flight.

Wild geese belong to wild places. Although no part of England

mary sewo

is either untamed or remote, there are times and surroundings which allow Nature to be herself again. Midwinter is such a time, the wide marshy plain of a river mouth such a place. Three days before Christmas, in iron weather, we have a day at duck, stepping out of time into eternity, out of civilisation into wilderness. Each man, day-long alone, has emptiness to look at but unending things to see, and even more to think about.

This is very different from the populous fellowship of the pheasant shoot. Collectively and severally, we eight shooters go through the day alone. We meet at the house, take a glass, and draw for our places. Our host tells each guest a thing or two about the lie of land and water, and what to expect. The headkeeper says, "Synchronise watches, gentlemen," and begins a count-down to "9.30 . . . now!" like an adjutant briefing column leaders before an attack. As adjutants also do, the headkeeper is staying behind, and there is just a suspicion of sooner-you-than-me in his parting glance as we walk out into the piercing air. We shoot from riverside hides, half-a-mile apart along the river bank. Interpreting bearing, shots and silences, we shall keep track of each other's doings, but we shall not see a human face until lunch. By winding lanes and then a cattle track, I drive within six hundred yards of my hide, park the car, load myself with gun and kit, call Hazel to my heel, and we walk out across water-meadows whitened by frost, through a rising mist, beneath a pale blue windless sky, while ice crackles under my feet like glass. I check my watch; eighteen minutes to ten o'clock. No need to hurry. Just as well, for I have a load to carry; gun, cartridge belt, binoculars, seat-stick, extra clothing (for warmth only, waterproofs will not be needed) and, more necessary than all except the gun, central heating.

This is a matter on which those who go out after duck have strongly held opinions. My choice is sloe gin. Others are of more innovative minds. Some believe that nothing equals whisky; some opt for cherry brandy, or just brandy; one in the party has a mixture of port and hare soup, another drinks rum and orange juice, both hot from vacuum flasks. What is not in dispute is the necessity. Frost is a temporary factor; symptom, not the cause of cold; just a dusting on the skin of the shivering earth.

We face a deeper chill. The world's latent heat has been withdrawn towards its core, and the same process draws the warmth from those who stand on its surface. When I stop walking I shall feel body-heat leaking away through my feet into the de-sensitised ground, and I shall need a restorative. My intake is less than that of some in this respect, but there is real pleasure in the weight of a belt-suspended flask bumping against my hip.

My hide is sited amid scrub. Though I have been to it before I do not at first see it. The scrub and all else is lost in the brilliant dazzle of frost. Stunted alders and willows, dead bulrush and reedmace are all rimed and sparkling as the sun's low rays penetrate the mist. Its refracted glare makes bearings difficult to find. Everything is as white and still as death except me, my dog, and the river – gun-metal grey as it slips along in a tight loop round a little promontory which contains the hide.

Three wattle panels form a rough triangle, with a gap left for entrance. Sprays of sallow have been stuffed into all three top edges to disguise the outline. Dog and I go inside. Our two extraneous figures disappear from the scene. I stow the goods and chattels, sample the central heating, load my gun, and check the time again.

Nobody must shoot before ten o'clock, however tempting the target. When somebody does shoot, the whole four miles of river will erupt with duck. For about a minute there will be duck within range, then twenty minutes without hope of a shot at all, and the rest of the morning at constant vigilance for a chance to take birds which, having been disturbed, are flighting back to home waters. If nobody shoots, presumably we shall wait indefinitely, frozen to inactivity from more than one cause. It is not a serious risk. I know who is No. 1 gun, furthest upstream. At No. 8, furthest downstream, I shall still be within his sphere of influence. For reasons long unfathomed, there is always something for him to shoot, no matter where the luck of the draw puts him.

The minute hand creeps up to twelve. Ten o'clock it is. I count ... one, two, three, four ... the time I estimate a gunshot's report to travel the distance the sound waves come. And there it is. Seconds later, two more, nearer at hand. Where I am, the local duck are slower to react. Hearing the first shot far away, they are alerted but not alarmed. When two more follow, indicating danger approaching, they take off. Three mallard come swinging down the line of the river, I swing the gun through, and press. The leading duck turns over in the air and falls dead in mid-water below us. The drake swerves, but my second barrel gets him, and he falls into some rushes on the far bank. Before I can re-load, eight more mallard and a single teal skim past.

At the first shot, Hazel darts from the hide. A flowing river is no place for such formalities as waiting for orders. She marked the splash of the falling mallard, and knows that it will be swept downstream fast. She is first airborne, then waterborne, and the greater splash as she hits the water almost drowns the second shot. A strong swimmer, she is soon at the spot where her ears told her the bird fell. Scent lies on water better than on land, and she picks it up instantly. She turns downstream, swims even faster, and after thirty yards turns back with the bird.

When she has delivered it she looks up at me for orders. She knows there was a second shot, but not the result of it. "Get over," I say. Another leap, another splash, another swim. At mid-stream she turns in the water to look back. I call, "Go on." When she climbs out on the other side the current has taken her well below where the drake is lying. Again she looks back. This time she is saying, "Give me a clue!" I signal her upstream. She gallops along the bank, sees the patch of rushes and pushes her way into it. Seconds later she is on her way back, mission accomplished.

In my kit I have a chamois leather, and rub her down. When I have dried and thawed-out my hands, and put my mittens on, I notice that drops of water above her eyes and on her ears have turned to ice. She does not care, and the river water is warmer than the air. I am reminded of the sloe gin. I drink it with one eye on the sky, the other ranging around.

For three miles in every direction the land would not need a contour on the map. It lies level under the remaining shreds of mist, far-off hills to the East, a line of fir woods to the West. A creaking in the air behind forewarns of swans in line astern. A flock of peewits flap soberly over, and settle to feed beyond the water. A robin perches on the hide, and looks boldly at the two immobile figures within. A bleak, isolated place for a robin, here in the loop of a river which will burst its banks before Winter is out, unsheltered in the bitter nights, with no windbreaks except rare leafless stems and the dry reeds rattling in their death. A cormorant, black and ragged and sinister, flies upstream to pillage young trout where the pools are deeper. At great height duck go by in fours and fives. The guns are silent. No man moves. Cattle have been taken to higher ground for fear of floods. The scene is empty and blank faced.

Into it, like a theme returning, come the unforgettable voices again. Geese are heading our way, coming down the valley from some feeding ground inland. When last I heard them, in the night, they were flying high, their cry as free as air. Now, flying low, the ground echo gives their voices deeper resonance. The clamour grows. I search its direction, but at first see nothing. Then, low against the horizon, a wide thin smudge is the line of the skein viewed head on, coming my way, calling, calling, purposeful and confident as marching soldiers. Soon they are overhead, I see the barred breasts of whitefronts, but not along the line of barrels. No shot of mine shall silence a single voice. They fly on inexorably, the long line growing thinner, the clanging voices fainter, until they are no more seen or heard.

Perhaps I shall see them again; on a cloudy, wind-torn mad March day, for instance. If the twentieth century roar abates for a few seconds their chorus may come down to me from overhead. If I crane my neck and focus for long sight I may just be lucky and glimpse them, Greenland-bound, on their return migration journey. Then there will be no wide thin line making a progress as implacable as a Roman legion, rolling out their tongues across pastures near below. They will be very high, almost at the limit of visibility, small swift arrowheads threading between cloud stacks as grey as they are, mastering the elements and, as ever, free.

But today, when they have gone, is past its zenith. After lunch we walk some frozen rushes for snipe, and for small reward. Most of the snipe have moved elsewhere. They need soft ground to probe for the invertebrate creatures which are their food. My bet is that they are nearer the farms than usual, as near as they can get to muck heaps which generate their own heat and seldom freeze, and are full of worms. Then we go back to our hides for evening flight. Nothing much happens while the light lasts, except a whole regiment of widgeon flying across the setting sun, a sun as red as our own frost-nipped faces, throwing a rosy light on the daylong rime. Then follows the ritual for the end of a winter's day, on this the shortest. The western colours fade, then intensify in a pulsating energy as day turns into night. The sun sinks behind the jagged fir wood. The sky turns from cold saffron to salmon pink, deepens to fiery red then amethyst, then purple which darkens until the curtain falls.

A gibous moon rises. The frost throws back her beams, so that the night sky is full of light. Limbs stiffened with cold and inactivity, eyes strained from watching, ears feeling the pinch of frost, hands frozen and trigger-fingers stiff, we wait on through the interlude of sterile beauty. Others are finding it sterile too. When the land freezes hard the ducks, which live by dabbling in shallows now hard ice, are forced towards deeper, moving water. The flock of widgeon, which had circled the area at sundown, now come our way again – magnetised by the moonlit river. Suddenly the still air is full of rushing wings; bodies sweep arrow-like across the canopy of stars. Guns are speaking, including mine; and Hazel responds to thud and splash. In ten minutes all is ended. It has been a long cold day for an average of five birds per gun. Hardly worth doing for the kill alone. We have gained something more when we come in, out of the night – a long look at diamond-hard Nature in the pitiless beauty of Winter.

TWO days later, Christmas Eve. The frost has not relented, and a north-east wind is rising. There is an ugly look of permanence about the weather from the North. Christmas is going to be all too white. While women wrap gifts, put up decorations, hang holly wreaths in doorways, switch-on the festive lights, men turn their hands outside. Straw bales are broken to bed down bullocks, sheep are brought close home, snow chains shackled to the wheels of Land-Rovers which take out feeds at dawn and dusk. Before the feasting and the worship end, we shall be in a state of seige, even here in Wessex, in the deep South. Only four inches of powdered snow is needed to block the downland roads with drifts, and cut us off for days.

Our festive season is more than symbolic. It combines the birth of Jesus with the Norse revels of our Saxon forbears; the Saviour with the pagan yule log and its unquenched flame;

things of the spirit with physical excess. So be it; we are as destiny has made us, our imperfections balanced by aspiration. From now until Plough Monday our ancestors blazed the trail of indulgence for two hectic weeks before they staggered forth again to win a living from the land. Our suspended animation is by comparison short-lived. Elsewhere there is no such interruption.

Beyond our warmth and shelter, under the snow and above it, life goes on. This single year has led me to the tracks of fox and deer, to rivers and sea, into sun and wind, into the ways of birds, and the majesty of trees and the mystery of small things. That which lives and inert matter are equally part of Creation. In briefly touching its small elements, in whatever cause, I have by chain-reaction made contact with all Creation, here and on the furthest star.

THE END

ACKNOWLEDGEMENTS

The author records his thanks to The Society of Authors as the literary representatives of the late John Masefield O.M., for their consent to the quotation of lines from *The Everlasting Mercy* and from *Reynard the Fox*. The lines by Adam Lindsay Gordon are from *How We Beat the Favourite*, those by Sir Walter Scott from *The Outlaw*, and those by Charles Hilton Brown from *Sawbath*. *Towards the East*, by Brigadier Bernard Fergusson later Lord Ballantrae, from which a stanza is quoted, was first published in 1945 by Collins, London, in a collection entitled *Lowland Soldier*. The opening quotation is from *The Soul Supreme* by Algernon Charles Swinburne.